# MIND THE GAP:

## NAVIGATING YOUR LEADERSHIP JOURNEY

by

**Doug Forsdick**
**Keri Schwebius**
**Heather Thomson**

A WOOD DRAGON BOOK

**Mind the Gap: Navigating Your Leadership Journey**

Cover design: Callum Jagger

**Published by:**
Wood Dragon Books
Post Office Box 429
Mossbank, Saskatchewan, Canada S0H3G0
www.wooddragonbooks.com

**Available in hardcover, paperback, eBook and audiobook**

**Library and Archives Canada Cataloguing in Publication**
Forsdick, Doug, 1967-
Schwebius, Keri, 1974-
Thomson, Heather, 1967-

ISBN: 978-1-989078-86-0 Hardcover
ISBN: 978-1-989078-84-6 Paperback
ISBN: 978-1-989078-87-7 eBook

**Author contact information**
Doug Forsdick - Victoria, British Columbia, Canada
doug.forsdick@gmail.com

Keri Schwebius - Regina, Saskatchewan, Canada
keri@ellevatecoaching.com

Heather Thomson - Sherwood Park, Alberta, Canada
boldandbravecoaching@gmail.com

# ■ Dedication ■

## DOUG

Thank you, Mom and Dad, Leah and Ateya, and those wonderful friends that have supported me along the way. Also, to those great leaders that I have worked with and learned so much from. You have all taught me and contributed to shaping me as I have taken my leadership journey. And last but not least … Anita. Thank you, without your support, I would not have been able to complete this book.

## KERI

Dedicated to my husband, Dean, and children, Katie, Laine and David who have supported me through my leadership journey and to my parents, Peter and Valerie who instilled in me strong values and leadership skills. Thank you to the wonderful leaders I had the pleasure of working for and learning from throughout my career—Bonnie, Robert, Joe, Wendy, Myrna, and Curt. Finally, to the amazing teams I had the pleasure of leading—your trust and feedback allowed me to grow.

## HEATHER

I am dedicating this book to my husband Derek and our daughter Cassidi who have always supported and encouraged me throughout my many endeavors. To my parents, Jim and Marg, who mean the world to me and who instilled in me my core values and my strong work ethic. To the amazing leaders that I have worked with and alongside who modeled what it means to be a leader. All of you have encouraged me to Dream Big, Set Goals, and Take Action.

# Contents

MANEUVER WITHIN YOUR ORGANIZATION

CONTINUE THE JOURNEY

# Note From The Authors

## DOUG FORSDICK

I spent the bulk of my 35 years in the public service specializing in the area of law enforcement. My career has been an amazing journey and one that I can say has never failed to interest, challenge, and fulfill me. In those 35 years, I have never had a day where I did not want to come to work. There were certainly days that were better than others, but I always had a desire to come to work and be part of an amazing team.

I have been exposed to some remarkable leaders that I have learned from along the way. You hear about some worksites or organizations that refer to themselves as a family. I can honestly say that the organization I am part of has become a family to me. I have lifelong friends as a result of my work in this field.

I set out on my career path following a family relative that did similar work. In my early years, he was somewhat of a hero to me, and I wanted to follow in his footsteps. When I entered this career, I never planned to rise through those ranks to be executive director / chief of the organization, but I am truly grateful everyday for that journey and what it has brought me.

I believe that I have had personal and organizational success because of one thing and one thing only—the people that make up our organization. I have had the absolute pleasure of being part of a team that is dedicated, capable, professional and completely engaged in their work. The work they do is challenging, at times insurmountable, often thankless, but so very rewarding and so extremely important.

My journey began in 1985 when I attended the British Columbia Institute of Technology and completed the Fish and Wildlife Program which focused on law enforcement. Unable to secure employment as a Conservation Officer, I found work at Oakalla Prison as a guard. Oakalla was known for its challenging conditions and notorious inmates. I began working there at the ripe age of 19, and I had to grow up quickly given who I was working with and who I was entrusted to keep safe and secure. Working at Oakalla Prison allowed me to see the other side of society and required me to begin my leadership journey.

I was eventually able to secure my dream job with the organization that I am still with today. My career has allowed me to carry out meaningful work and to truly make a difference. I have been exposed to major and complex investigations, new and exciting initiatives and some very dangerous encounters. I have progressed from a front-line officer to a leader responsible for those fine men and women that carry the badge and do the great work that they do.

I have had the opportunity to be president of the North American Wildlife Enforcement Officers Association, which is an association representing over 8000 members. I am currently the president of Canadian Natural Resource Law Enforcement Chiefs Association. These opportunities have allowed me to grow as a leader. They have each exposed me to different challenges and opportunities and most importantly to a variety of interesting and wonderful people that I have learned leadership skills from.

In addition to career related opportunities, I have been fortunate to represent British Columbia at the national level as the president of the provincial sport organization—Biathlon BC. This role has provided me with many opportunities to ensure the sport of Biathlon was promoted and supported in British Columbia, and to ensure that biathletes were well represented at the national level. The organization is extremely diverse. My role was to support all levels of the sport from grass roots to high performance, including those athletes representing Canada internationally. The many learnings and opportunities at Biathlon BC have helped me to learn and grow as a leader.

As I completed my 30th year with my employer, I decided that I wanted to challenge myself by taking a more formalized approach to leadership coaching by enrolling in the Royal Roads Executive Coaching program. The end of my formal career with the public service was fast approaching, and I truly wanted to give back. I felt that I had much to offer both from my successes and from those times when I was not so successful but had learned from the experience. I wanted to use structured coaching to help others.

While at Royal Roads, I met my co-authors Keri and Heather. I was immediately drawn to these two remarkable women for their strength, sense of humour, knowledge and experience, and their wonderful attitudes toward leadership and personal growth. We soon developed a strong and rich friendship. I can't think of two people I would rather collaborate with on a book as I appreciate their many experiences and learnings that have contributed so richly to this book.

I am forever indebted to those leaders that shaped who I am as a leader and a person today. They have benefitted me more than they will ever know.

## KERI SCHWEBIUS

For more than 20 years, I worked in corporate communications helping executive teams communicate with stakeholders. During this time, I was a messenger, a translator and an advisor for leaders. This 20-year experience led me to further engage in the field of leadership, first as a leader, then later empowering others to become leaders. My passion for leadership ultimately led me to complete a Master of Arts in Leadership and a Graduate Certificate in Executive Coaching, both at Royal Roads University in Victoria, British Columbia.

My leadership journey has provided me with wonderful experiences where great leaders have allowed me to grow and thrive.

For example, I had a boss, Robert, who inherited me when our teams were merged into one after my previous manager left the company. He and I had different areas of expertise. He was a pro in compensation while I was a writer and communicator. He gave me the opportunity to work on a performance management strategy for a major client. I had never taken on a task like that before, but he provided me with all the tools I needed as well as the time to work on it. He empowered me to take on something new, to learn and grow from the experience, and to offer value to an important client. For me, he was a great leader.

But I've also had many experiences over my career where the poor leadership of others has limited me. For example, I had a boss, Mitch, who let six months pass without meeting with me. I had no direction or information from him, while he had no idea what I was working on nor what opportunities or challenges I might be facing.

While my formal training has allowed me to become very skilled at leadership, my work experience has taught me about the kind of leadership that allows employees to really thrive.

When I started my master's degree, we were placed into triads, groups of three people who would support and challenge each other through the two-year program. One evening, I was working with my triad in my dorm room. In the small space, I was sitting on the bed while my triad members sat on chairs as we discussed why we were there and what we planned to do with our degrees. When it came to me, I jumped up on the bed, threw my arms in the air and said, "I want to change the world."

I wanted to help other people become the kind of leaders who support their employees to thrive. I wanted to be a Robert, not a Mitch—and help other people to do the same.

The world can be a difficult place. People face much adversity and suffering. We can't begin to understand the challenges people are facing every day. Life is hard. But—it can also be wonderful, joyful and amazing. As we spend much of our time at work, imagine if our workplaces contributed to people's happiness and life satisfaction.

Great leaders can make this happen. As a leader, you have a choice. You can create a team or workplace that contributes to misery and discontent or you can create a team where people feel valued, supported and invested in the success of your organization.

I wrote this book with my colleagues to help people do the latter. We are better when we work together. In fact, I started writing this book before I met Heather and Doug, but I never gained enough momentum to complete the project. When the three of us started sharing ideas, setting deadlines and supporting each other, we were able to achieve what I wasn't able to on my own.

It takes work to be a great leader. It takes a concerted effort to first work on yourself, your skills, self-awareness, wellness and behaviours.

Then it takes even more effort to work on the relationships with those who report to you, and finally to navigate the organizations in which you are employed.

Along with Heather and Doug, I wrote this book to help people become better leaders. I want leaders to feel what it's like to create a workplace where employees are not only happy and productive, but thriving and achieving results previously thought impossible.

## HEATHER THOMSON

I have worked in the field of education for over 27 years and am just as passionate about my profession as I was when I began my career. Over the years, I have had the opportunity to teach in two countries and three provinces and have loved every minute of it. I have learned many things along the way that have shaped the person I have become. I have a strong passion and love for learning and embrace any opportunity that I can to learn and implement new things.

My formal education includes: a Bachelor of Business Administration, a Masters in Counselling Psychology, a Masters in Educational Leadership, a Secondary Teaching Certificate, and Graduate Executive Coaching Certificate. I am a Certified Positive Intelligence Coach and received my designation through the Positive Intelligence Institute. As well, I hold an Associate Certified Coaching Designation through the International Coaching Federation and am a trained facilitator in Personality Dimensions.

During my time as an educator, I have held various positions that helped to shape and guide me on my leadership journey. My career began as a classroom teacher and over the years my roles have changed. I was an Inclusive Learning Facilitator, School Counsellor, Department Head, and High School Administrator. In each of these positions, I had the opportunity to stretch and grow myself as a visionary leader.

For the last several years, I have been a High School Administrator and have worked in two different communities in Alberta. My work in my leadership role was rewarding and I had many opportunities to coach staff. However, with my passion for lifelong learning, I wanted to learn more about coaching and the positive impact it could have not only on my leadership skills but on those team members

I worked with. In 2019, I enrolled in the Executive Coaching program at Royal Roads. As a strong believer in lifelong learning and personal development—whether it be by reading a book, attending a workshop, taking a course, or just collaborating with other leaders—the coaching program at Royal Roads ignited a spark in me that has been truly life changing.

Throughout my leadership journey, I wished I had more opportunities to be coached and mentored. Like many leaders I work with, we learn the role by trial and error. This is one of the reasons I wanted to write this book as a resource for people to use on their leadership journey.

I met Doug and Keri at Royals Roads while we were enrolled in the Graduate Executive Coaching program and we immediately became friends. We all shared the same passion for coaching and wanted to support leaders on their leadership journey. When Doug, Keri and I decided to write this book, we brainstormed key areas that we felt were important in supporting a leader on their journey. As we began to write, we continued to add additional chapters that we felt were missing and that was how "Mind the Gap: Navigating Your Leadership Journey" was created.

Like many new leaders, I remember how nervous I was in my first leadership role as a department head. Although I understood the role of the department head, I realized there were many things I still needed to learn. As a new leader, many thoughts raced through my mind—some of excitement and some of sheer terror. I worried what people might think if I made a mistake. What if I gave someone the wrong answer? How would I deal with a difficult conversation with a member on the team? In my *Mental Fitness Coaching* training through Positive Intelligence, we call these racing thoughts our *saboteur tendencies* because they create an internal dialogue in our minds that leads to doubts, stress and worries. These thoughts can hold you back from reaching your true potential.

One of the requirements in applying for my first leadership position was to have started or completed a master's degree program. I did my first master's degree through San Diego State University which had partnered with Burnaby School District in British Columbia to offer a Master of Arts in Educational Leadership. The program was amazing, and I gained many insights into being an educational leader; however, I still had a great deal to learn about the leadership role itself. As a leader, there are many dynamics at play when one leads a team or organization.

Although I came off as confident in my new role as department head, I definitely had some *Imposter Syndrome* issues going on in the beginning. Like many new leaders, I was worried about whether or not I was qualified enough, had enough experience, training or education to do the job effectively. I was waiting for someone to come and say that I was a fraud or I was not experienced enough for the role.

At the time, I was one the youngest department heads in our school and was on a team of seasoned department heads. They were amazing to work with and supported me in my new role. My school-based team was extremely hard working and we worked collaboratively together to successfully grow our programs and department. As I became more comfortable in my role, I realized that as a new leader, I was not the only one who had felt Imposter Syndrome in the beginning of their leadership journey. Many of us know the technical aspect of the role; however, leading a team is quite different. I appreciated the mentorship and guidance from the other department heads as well as from my principal and assistant principals.

My learning journey continued to focus both on my professional and my personal development. These two areas are interconnected. As part of my learning journey, co-authoring this book has allowed me to reflect on my own personal leadership journey and share my thoughts. If I were to give advice to my younger self, I would tell her three things:

1. Set clear goals that align with your core values.
2. Do not be afraid to fail. When we fail, we are learning and growing.
3. Work with a Leadership Coach.

As a leader, I would have loved a book like this as I began my leadership journey. The leader I was 20 years ago is not the leader that I am today.

# ■ Introduction ■

There is a gap between being an employee and being a leader. The skills you need to be successful as an employee are not the same skills you need to lead other people. Yet being promoted to a leadership position is often a reward for being great at one's job.

Many new leaders make the leap from being highly proficient and, confident in their non-management roles to suddenly being responsible for the success of others. More often than not, this happens with no additional training or support. Think of it this way—before you became a (enter your profession/job here) you had some sort of training, whether it was formal or on-the-job. In many cases, this training included two to four years of attending lectures, writing research papers and exams, all focused on preparing you to become a professional. Then suddenly, you're promoted to a leadership position and a whole new set of skills is required. Likely, you didn't go back to school two to four more years to learn those new skills required to be successful in this new role. If you're lucky, your organization has a leadership development program in place—

but many organizations don't, so new managers are left to their own devices.

We have taken that leap. In combination, we have spent decades learning to be leaders. Among the three of us, we have worked in a broad scope of organizations and industries, including law enforcement, education, healthcare, oil and gas, financial services, non-profit, publicly funded, private, and co-operative. We have led small teams in one location and large teams spanning several locations. We have also experienced how good leadership can positively affect people, teams and organizations just as poor leadership can have a negative, sometimes even devastating effect. No matter the organization, the industry or the structure, regardless of the issues or challenges, the skills required to be an effective leader are the same across the board.

In this book, we share the experiences and insights we have acquired about leadership. The things we have learned through: formal education, such as master's degrees and post-graduate certificates in executive coaching; certifications, like Prosci change management and Emotional Intelligence; and on-the-job experiences and observations—have been pulled together in one place to support others to fill the gap and make the leap from being a great employee to becoming an effective leader.

This book is organized in four main areas of leadership:

***Focus on you.*** Leadership starts with you. Before you can even begin to influence others as a leader, you need to understand who you are, what drives you, and how your behaviours impact others. Without the ability to look at yourself and reflect on your strengths and opportunities, you will never be fully equipped to lead others.

***Plot the course and steer the way.*** The second section of the book focuses on leading other people. You must develop and nurture connections and relationships with the people you lead. Even though you have been given a position of authority, you must earn the privilege to lead others. In this section of the book, we look at integral leadership skills like building trust and effectively communicating.

***Maneuver within your organization.*** You are part of an organization, an industry, and a community. The third section looks at what it takes to lead a team within this context.

***Continue the journey.*** Finally, learning how to be an effective leader never ends. The people we lead and the context within which we lead them is always changing. That's why we describe leadership as a journey. As you move forward on your leadership journey, you will have opportunities to stop and reflect on your experience.

As we introduce each topic, we discuss what it means, why it's important for leaders and, most importantly, how to do it. We finish each chapter with reflection questions. While the skills for leaders are the same, you will have your own leadership style. The reflection questions help you, the reader, consider how you will approach your leadership journey.

We believe everyone deserves to work with a strong leader. Although the world and our lives are filled with many struggles and challenges, we cannot control—as leaders, we have the power to create workplaces where people feel valued and where they believe they can contribute and make a difference.

We wrote this book to help you become a better leader and contribute to positive and constructive workplaces. Take a moment to reflect and consider these questions before continuing to read.

1. What kind of leader do I want to be?
2. What do I want people to say about my leadership?
3. Who are the leaders I've loved working with? What was it about their leadership that I liked? How can I imitate those positive behaviours in my own work?
4. If I am a better leader tomorrow than I am today, what difference would that make for me? For the people who work with me? For the organization I'm part of?

Your journey will have many twists, turns, and even detours along the way. Use these experiences as if they are gifts—opportunities that will guide you on your journey. Learn to be adaptable and flexible, and continue to push yourself in your leadership role. As you grow, the leader you are today will probably look very different from the leader you will become. Embrace the journey and strive towards always being the best version of yourself and the leader you aspire to be.

# Leaders versus Managers

*"He who thinks he leads, but has no followers, is only taking a walk."*

*John Maxwell, bestselling author on leadership*

Leadership thought leader John Kotter, writing in the Harvard Business Review, pointed out the fundamental differences between leading and managing. According to Kotter, a manager tends to follow the vision, stays true to policies and procedures, and follows the organization's road map. A leader tends to be more involved in setting the vision, exploring possibilities, and going "off-road" to explore uncharted territory.

In other words, managers are inclined to focus on "how" things get done, while the leaders tend to focus on "what" needs to be done, creating the vision and forward thinking. Managers stay true to the organization's goals and ensure the team reaches its target. They do this mainly through five management functions: planning, organizing, staffing, directing and controlling. All of these are more directive in nature and leave little room for feedback from the team.

Managers will focus on the status quo and keep practices as they have been in the past, often giving rise to responses such as, "Because we have always done it like that."

Leaders, on the other hand, encourage their team to create ideas and thoughts that stretch a person outside their comfort zone to help the team reach their goals faster. Leaders truly believe that with collaboration and sharing of ideas, magic can happen. It is the leader's responsibility to build a culture of trust within the team where all ideas are valued and appreciated. The team will not be afraid to go "off-road" or build a road to a new destination if their leader has built a strong culture of trust.

Leaders encourage the team to get curious and seek out new possibilities and ideas that align with the organization's values, vision and mission. They work collaboratively with their team to see what actions or steps are needed today that will help move the organization toward its future goals. Leaders encourage their teams to dream big and look at potential future opportunities. Leaders stretch themselves and others around them to think outside of the box. They believe that no idea is a bad idea and will put everything on the table. Leaders look for ways to continually improve the system and are not afraid to challenge the status quo.

In the early 2000s, leaders were encouraged to be "change agents." In Stephen Covey's book, *The 7 Habits of Highly Effective People*, he captured this shift very adeptly and focused on how leaders could be more effective in their roles. Covey shared a jungle analogy to demonstrate the difference between leading and managing: the leaders are the ones who are using machetes to cut their way through the jungle and the managers are behind them making sure the machetes are sharpened, the team has the required supplies, and everyone has a clear understanding of where and why they are heading in that direction. At certain times, the leaders will stop and climb the trees in the jungle to make sure that they are still heading in the direction they want to go. Sometimes, the leader will choose another path in mid-stream, pivot and go in another direction, even if the manager feels that things are moving along satisfactorily. The leader is not afraid to yell out, "Wrong Jungle!"

Peter Drucker and Warren Bennis, two well-known experts in the field of management, state that leadership is doing the right thing and management is doing things right. Similar to Stephen Covey's jungle analogy, the leader sets and creates the shared vision and the manager ensures that the team is following it out.

There are times when a person will need to lead and times when a person will need to manage. A leader is rarely able to do both at the same time, as leading and managing are different skill sets and they are required at different times. A prime example are school principals. Some tasks they do will require them to take on the leadership role while other tasks will require them to take on a managerial role. At the time of this writing, Heather's school division has a school assurance plan that is referred to throughout the year for guidance in their practice moving forward. The team, under the leadership of the principal, builds school goals aligned with district goals. The principal, along with the help of his assistant principals, are responsible to lead the school and ensure the school's and district's vision align. The principal, in his or her management role, manages staffing, timetabling and budgeting. As you can see, the principal straddles between the leadership and management roles.

No matter where you are on your leadership journey, it is important to understand the difference between being a leader versus being a manager. In your leadership role, there will be times when you wear your leadership hat but there will also be times when you wear your manager hat. Be clear on what those differences look like for your organization and how you would do both roles. Today's leadership role encompasses both aspects to varying degrees and it becomes a bit of a graceful dance—moving from leader to manager as needed—allowing for a smooth ease and flow.

## HEATHER'S EXPERIENCE

*When I was in my third year in a leadership role, a retired principal shared with me this advice. He said, "Take a moment and envision yourself at your retirement party. Think about what you would want people to say about you as their leader. What would they share about your leadership style and how have you impacted them as a leader?"*

## ▤ REFLECTION QUESTIONS ▤

1.  Think about your favourite boss. What leadership skills did they demonstrate?

2.  What management skills are important in my role?

3.  What leadership skills are important in my role?

4.  In what situations should I draw on management skills versus leadership skills and vice versa?

5.  Which skills do I demonstrate more often in my work? Leadership skills? Management skills?

# Values – Your Bottom Line

**"If You Don't Stand for Something, You'll Fall for Anything."**

*Author Unknown*

Rooted in our upbringing and our past experiences, our values shape how we respond to the world and the decisions we make. While people may have similar values, values are very personal and the same value can show up differently in individuals' behaviours.

As a leader, it's important to know what you stand for and what values guide your decisions. Life is rarely simple, especially when humans are involved. People are emotional and complicated. There's often no perfect solution to a complex problem involving employees. However, clearly articulated values give you a framework for decision making. As a leader struggling with complex decisions, being clear about your values can help you make difficult decisions with the confidence that those decisions align with your values. When you know what's most important to you and understand how you want a particular value to show up through your actions, you can ensure that what you do is in line with what you believe. In addition, when you are clear in your values, your employees will know what to expect from you. They'll be able to discern whether or not their own values align with yours.

Let's suppose one of your values is courage. At various times in your life and as a leader, the value of courage will guide you. You will speak up when you see someone being treated poorly. You will take risks even when you're scared. You will make bold changes in your life and workplace even if you're not guaranteed a positive outcome.

Another value you hold might be gratitude. If you value gratitude, you may choose to find the positive in any situation. When an employee leaves you for a new opportunity, you may be upset they left you in a tight spot. When you lean on your values, you will be grateful for their contributions during the time they were with you. This value will directly impact your attitude, which in turn will be reflected in your behaviours. Rather than treating that employee with anger and frustration, you'll show them appreciation and wish them well.

## ARTICULATED VALUES CREATE CLARITY FOR YOU AND THE PEOPLE WHO WORK WITH YOU

When you've taken the time to understand and articulate what's most important to you, you create clarity for yourself as well as your employees. Leaders working with a new team should share a little bit about themselves and their background, including their values. When a leader is clear about his or her values and shares them with the team, the employees know what to expect. It also helps them decide if their new leader is the kind of boss they want to work for.

For example, consider a leader who values family. That person might allow themselves to be called away from work to pick up a sick child from school or take time off to watch their child's talent show or school play. That leader would also allow employees the same flexibility without judgement.

You will attract people with similar values and together you can create shared values for your organization. Shared values drive the way your company treats employees, customers and other stakeholders. When an organization shares their corporate values with the public, they allow potential employees to consider whether their own personal values align. This is a first step in screening out potential employees who will ultimately fail in your organization because of a misalignment of values. Similarly, when an employee believes their personal values align with the company's values, they are more likely to stay with the organization and be more engaged in contributing towards achieving the company's vision.

It's important to ensure the values your company is articulating align with the behaviours your leaders are demonstrating. If leaders don't "walk the talk," employees won't either.

## WHEN YOUR VALUES COMPETE

Conflicting values can create dilemmas. You may value family as well as financial stability. Perhaps you work 70 hours a week to ensure financial stability and provide for your family. However, while you are working for your family, you have little time left to spend with them. This is true for many parents. If you are clear about your values, you can find opportunities to balance them. For example, in this scenario, you may create more quality time instead of quantity. If you only have a few hours with your family in a week, you might choose to give them your undivided attention during those hours.

Stress can affect how your values show up. You're human and sometimes your behaviours won't align with your values. This is particularly true when you're under stress. If you've ever snapped at someone for no good reason, you've experienced this. You're not always your most perfect self when you're dealing with big challenges, tight timelines, fatigue or grief.

The best way to deal with these instances is to apologize and learn from the experience. Ask yourself how you could have behaved differently. Could you reduce the stress in your life? If your behaviour is consistently misaligned with your values, it might be time to make some changes.

## WHEN YOUR VALUES ARE GETTING IN THE WAY OF YOUR HAPPINESS

If you're living and behaving in a way that is true to your values, but you're unhappy, consider revisiting those values. You may be putting value on the wrong things or you may not be clear about what those values mean for you. Success is a good example. Success can mean different things to different people, especially looking in from the outside. You can have success in one area of your life, your career for example, but still feel something is missing. When this is the case, take a step back, revisit your values and make changes.

When you are clear about your values, when your behaviours align with those values, and when you're satisfied with how your values contribute to your overall happiness, you will be a better, more effective leader.

When your values don't align with the person you work for, or the organization as a whole, it's likely not the right place for you.

## KERI'S EXPERIENCE

*Early in my leadership studies, I did an exercise to articulate my values. I thought I had pretty strong values that guided my behaviours, but I had never put a name to them or thought about what they meant to me.*

*Many years prior to that we were having a staff celebration where I worked. A small group of about seven or eight of us, some managers, others non-management, were gathered around a large table in an Executive Vice President's office. Some of us reported up through her. I did not. Being in that office was intimidating. I had just recently been promoted to manager and wanted to make a good impression.*

*The meeting started with the goal to plan an event that would be fun and entertaining for our employees. The company was receiving an award for being a great workplace. The EVP wanted to make sure the employees knew they were a large part of creating this success. She wanted them to feel recognized and rewarded.*

*I don't recall who came up with the idea, but we started to talk about creating a parody of American Idol. We thought it would be fun to have some of our employees impersonate the panel of judges like the one on the television reality show. At the time, the judges panel included Simon Cowell, Randy Jackson, Steven Tyler and Jennifer Lopez. Some people stepped up to take on the roles. An Associate Vice President who reported directly to the EVP would play Steven Tyler. Some jokes were made about eyeliner. A really tall, smart and extroverted manager would play J Lo. Then someone suggested another manager play the part of Randy Jackson.*

*That's when things started to get uncomfortable for me. As plans were made, there was talk about using makeup to make our white employee look like Randy Jackson, an African American man. At the time there wasn't a single Black Canadian employed at the company. Diversity was never a strength in the organization. As I looked around the room, I saw that no one else seemed to be uncomfortable. I started to second-guess myself. Was I being too sensitive? I didn't want to be the only voice of dissent in the group. I was a new manager. I was trying to make a good impression. How could I do that by telling this group of people their idea was racist?*

*I left the meeting feeling slightly ill. This meeting dominated my thoughts and actions for the next several days. I needed to do something. First, I spoke briefly to the employee who was volun-told to play Randy. He informed me that he wasn't comfortable with it and would be playing Simon Cowell instead. He said he just thought about what his black friends would think of him playing a black man (with make-up) and didn't think they'd look very favourably on it.*

*Next, I spoke with a woman in Human Resources. I trusted her. She and I had many conversations where we shared our honest perspectives on things so I knew I could talk to her about what I was thinking and feeling. Apparently, at the time, not everyone was familiar with blackface and the significant historical reasons why it is so absolutely offensive. She set up a meeting with the EVP, herself and I to discuss the issue further.*

*Before heading to that meeting, I decided it was important to let my boss, another EVP, know what was going on. I popped my head into his office and asked for a minute. He invited me in. We didn't sit. I didn't want to take up too much of his time. I quickly blurted out the details of the situation and how I was in conflict with another EVP. I didn't even give him an opportunity to tell me I was wrong (I knew I wasn't). I told him that I didn't need anything from him, I just wanted to let him know what was going on.*

*The meeting was in the HR offices, around a much smaller table, more intimate but still intimidating. I explained to the EVP that what we would be doing is called blackface and provided her the history around it. I explained that it's very offensive and encouraged her to make sure we didn't do it. The woman in human resources said there were now two employees who were not comfortable with the plan and perhaps we should consider not painting anyone's face. The executive argued that another EVP wore make-up the previous Halloween when she dressed up as Michael Jackson. (As if the fact that an executive had done this made it acceptable.) The EVP seemed unconvinced but finally conceded. I was relieved. Even if she didn't agree with me (and millions of people around the world) at least she wasn't going to allow it to happen.*

*I left that meeting still unsure of myself. Was I out of line? What kind of impression had I left on this woman who had so much power in my organization? Why was putting black make-up on someone so important to her? Did she think the event would be any less fun? But at least I had stopped it.*

The next day, I was walking from the elevator back to my office when the woman from HR caught me in the hallway. She had spoken to the EVP again. The EVP went to the CEO about what had now become "the issue" and he didn't see anything wrong with using make-up to change someone's race, so they were going to go ahead with it. My stomach dropped. I'm sure my face went red. I thought this situation was resolved. The CEO was an educated man, a lawyer. I could not fathom the thought that he had no knowledge of blackface. "What?" I said to her, incredulous. She just shrugged her shoulders, surrendering to the reality that the EVP always gets her way, whether or not it's right.

I was furious, frustrated, and frankly—scared. I needed someone to validate my feelings. I went to a co-worker who I knew would be informed enough to understand what the problem was. She had a cubicle so I had to keep my voice low so others couldn't hear us. I leaned on her desk and disclosed to her what was about to take place. It was probably out of line for me to be talking to her about it, but I felt like a crazy person. I wanted to be assured I wasn't crazy. She was disgusted. She told me if it happened, she would walk out of the event in protest.

While her support was reassuring, it didn't solve the problem. I knew what was going on and I made it my responsibility to educate my leaders and ultimately prevent it from happening. I found myself in a very uncomfortable place. I was a fairly new middle manager, and I was disagreeing with an executive. I contemplated what I would do if my concerns were ignored, and we actually put someone in blackface. Would I need to walk away from my job? I just got this job. It was a great company. I had a great team. I had a family to support. I was happy to be there but how could I work for a company when their senior leaders' actions were ignorant and disrespectful?

I went home that night and, after getting my kids fed and put to bed and debriefing my husband on the issue, took one last shot at putting a halt to the blackface plans. I sat cross-legged on my living room couch, sitcoms playing in the background, laptop in front of me and I wrote what I hoped would be a very compelling email. I spent more than an hour on it and read it at least 30 times. I provided the history of blackface and why it's offensive. I linked to articles where high-profile people had been called out in the press for blackface. I said I would not defend the company if anyone in or out of our organization was offended by it. Since I was in charge of media relations, I might have been in a position to do so. Finally, I suggested that if the organization granting us an award for being a great workplace were to discover we were putting someone in blackface, we might lose our award.

I didn't send the email that night. I had my husband read it over to make sure I wasn't saying anything inappropriate or offensive. I let it settle while I *slept. The next morning as soon as I arrived at the office, I read the email one last time and hit send. I worried about the consequences of pushing my opposing position so hard, especially upward in the hierarchy. I worried about losing my job or having to make the difficult decision to leave voluntarily. I worried about the consequences of what I had done, but I didn't worry about what I had done.*

*Thankfully, that final effort worked. The EVP dropped the issue. No one wore blackface. The event turned out really fun—for everyone. That was probably about the time I started to realize I wasn't a good fit for the organization, or it wasn't a good fit for me, although it would still be some time before I left. A few years later, yet another celebrity landed in the news for going in blackface at Halloween.*

*The next time I was in the EVP's office, she said,*

*"Do you remember that time we did the American Idol thing?"*

*What? Of course, I do. It's ingrained in my memory for eternity. I tell the story at parties.*

*"Yes," I said out loud.*

*"That was good advice," she told me.*

*Had I been really clear about my values at that point in time, it may have been very easy for me to say to myself, "If they do this, I'm out. I will quit my job, because it doesn't align with my value of respect for everyone."*

*The gut feeling I had at the time pointed me in the right direction and I'm proud of how hard I pushed. Being really solid in what your values are and what they mean to you makes it much easier to make decisions.*

## VALUES GUIDE YOUR ACTIONS, ESPECIALLY WHEN YOU SAY THEM OUT LOUD

Create a template, similar to the following example, to help you articulate your own values. This may be a simple exercise for some values and more difficult for others. Take your time and refine them as you consider what they mean to you and the behaviours you want to exhibit. You might start with a long list and then narrow it down, combining some and being really clear about others.

Two examples of Keri's values:

| What do I value? | What does that mean to me? | Why is this my bottom line? | What does this look like in my actions? |
|---|---|---|---|
| Family | The health, wellbeing and happiness of my family is a priority for me. | I am responsible for the care and nurturing of my children as well as positively influencing their development into independent adults. I've also made a commitment to my husband that we will do this as a team. | I am a positive example for my children in the hopes of instilling my values in them.<br><br>I will dedicate time and energy to my children's growth and development. I will take time to play with them, help them with schoolwork and give them experiences that help them grow. |
| Respect | I treat people with dignity and respect, valuing their contributions and viewpoints, regardless of gender, race, title or other attributes. | I believe every life is precious and every person has the potential to bring value to any situation. | I will seek to understand others.<br><br>I stop myself when I make assumptions about someone else. I ask questions to learn their truth. |

## ■ REFLECTION QUESTIONS ■

1. How will articulating my values help me to be a better leader?

2. What do I value?

3. What does this value mean to me?

4. Why is this value important?

5. What does this look like in my actions? How will my employees see this in my behaviours?

6. What might indicate I'm slipping away from this value?

# MIND THE GAP

# Finding Your Purpose

*"Always go with your passions. Never ask yourself if it is realistic or not."*

**Deepak Chopra, Author of The Seven Spiritual Laws of Success**

Sometimes as we begin our leadership journey, we may be struck by Imposter Syndrome, where we don't fully believe that we qualify or deserve the role we find ourselves in. When we share our lack of confidence with others, we might get the advice, "Fake it 'til you make it." This guidance might work for skill development, pretending we can do what needs to be done until we have enough experience or training to do so competently. But what cannot be faked is understanding our purpose.

As a leader, having a clearly defined purpose is an important part of your leadership journey. It is your internal compass that tells you why you want to be a leader and how you want to show up as one. With a strong sense of purpose, you are clear about what your core values, strengths, and passions are.

Knowing your purpose drives your behavior and allows you to lead more intentionally. It allows you to deal with Imposter Syndrome because you know you are exactly where you should be, regardless of your learning curve ahead. Aligning your purpose with your actions will create professional fulfillment in your role as leader.

## HOW DO YOU KNOW WHAT YOUR PURPOSE IS?

Understanding your purpose, clearly defining your how and why, requires an investment of your time. Knowing what your strengths, passions, and values are and how you use these gifts and talents to navigate your leadership career is important to have top of mind as you self-reflect. What do you love about being a leader? Living your purpose in your professional life is about getting up in the morning and being excited about going to work. It means feeling energized and passionate in your leadership role and recognizing your work is a career and not a job.

As you reflect on your leadership journey, begin to think about what you are truly passionate about, what would make you excited to leap out of bed every day. If someone asked you tomorrow to share your leadership purpose, could you clearly state what it is? What is your how and why of leadership? Articulating your purpose is not an easy process; it takes time and self-reflection to identify your purpose statement.

If you are struggling to begin, think about when you were a child. What did you love to do? Did you feel called to something? What were you passionate about? You may be surprised to see common themes throughout your life.

### HEATHER'S EXPERIENCE

*When I was a young child, I knew I wanted to be an educator. I would invite all of the neighbourhood kids over to my house and we would play 'school.' My mom would help me organize field trips for 'my students' and these experiences are some of my fondest memories. I have always loved helping others which led me down a winding road to education.*

*When I graduated from high school, I took Office Education at the Saskatchewan Technical Institute or STI (now called Saskatchewan Polytechnic) in Moose Jaw. Many of my female high school classmates enrolled in this program and boy did we have a fun time. After completing that program, I worked at CIBC for a few years as a bank teller and really enjoyed meeting and interacting with people. During that time, the bank partnered with the University of Regina, offering satellite Business Courses for first year university classes. I enrolled in a course. I did surprisingly well so I then applied to Nipissing University in North Bay, Ontario where I earned a Bachelor of Business Administration degree. I was heading down the path to become a Certified Management Accountant (CMA).*

*You are probably asking yourself how I ended up getting my teaching degree. Life has a funny way of steering you towards your true calling. During my last year of my degree, I dated a fellow going through the Education program. It sounded so interesting. I began to do some research and knew that this career was what I was called to do. To be a servant leader and to serve and support others. It aligned with my core values and life's purpose. At around that time, my dad, who was in the military, was transferred to Colorado Springs to work at NORAD. Much to my surprise they had a teaching certification program at Regis University in Colorado so off I went to become a teacher. Moving to Colorado with my family allowed me to live at home while still attending the teaching program which saved me a lot of money.*

*It has been 27 years since I began my education journey and, even to this day, I still get energized by being in the classroom or coaching teachers as part of my role as administrator. My transition into coaching leaders has aligned perfectly with my core values and beliefs, strengths and work-life experience. Clarity and a sense of purpose have guided me on my leadership journey.*

## WHEN YOUR CAREER DOES NOT ALIGN WITH YOUR PURPOSE

Working in a career that aligns with your purpose is important to your overall well being. Sometimes individuals say they have a "calling" to their career—they have been called to or drawn to their work. Others share that they were clear on what they are passionate about earlier on in life and this clarity led them to their career. Whatever steps lead you to your calling are part of finding your purpose.

If you work in a career that does not align with your purpose, you can still be successful; however, your work may not be something that you love doing. Success and happiness do not necessarily go hand in hand. When we set goals for ourselves it does not mean that we will be fulfilled when we reach that goal. For example, you may have a goal to make a six-figure income. Achieving that goal does not mean you will be happy, but setting and achieving a goal that you want to make a six-figure income in a career that you love may in fact give you both success and happiness.

## NOW WHAT?

Finding your purpose, understanding your why, or knowing your personal mission statement are important on your leadership journey. Your personal experiences help shape who you are and how you will find your true passion. Staying open and curious is part of the journey of self-discovery. When you find your purpose, work does not seem like work. Your purpose is not defined by your job title or degrees that you hold. It is about who you truly aspire to be and what you're passionate about. Your life is more fulfilling when you are clear about what is important to you.

Knowing your purpose provides you with clarity, a sense of passion, and living a more fulfilling life filled with happiness and joy.

### ▓ REFLECTION QUESTIONS ▓

1. What activities am I engaged in when I lose track of time?
2. What activities make me feel energized?
3. When do I feel the happiest and most fulfilled?
4. What steps do I need to take in order to create a clear and concise purpose?
5. Why is it important for my team to be aware of my purpose?
6. What can I do to keep my purpose "top of mind," even when my role as leader is challenging?

# Showing Up As a Leader

*"Leadership is about making others better as a result of your presence and making sure that impact lasts in your absence."*

**Sheryl Sandberg, former Chief Operating Officer, Facebook**

Some believe a strong and impactful leader is one that has a "leadership presence." This is about being engaged, being accessible, being true to your word. The critical piece of leadership presence is ensuring that you are a *positive presence*.

Some feel you need to be that outgoing leader that rallies the team and charges at the front of the pack. There is no doubt that some enjoy working for that strong, bold and confident leader. There are, however, other leadership styles that lend themselves to greater outcomes, depending on the team, the people involved, and the environments.

Whichever style you have now or you mold to make your own, it is critical that you show up as a leader with a style that is your own and that makes an impact on others.

## AUTHENTIC STYLE

### DOUG'S EXPERIENCE

*Retired Canadian General and Chief of Defence Rick Hillier says the two greatest attributes of a leader are optimism and toughness. I couldn't agree more with General Hillier. I have modelled my leadership style from General Hillier's and bring optimism and toughness to everything I do as a leader. My definition of toughness does not mean a lack of empathy or caring, it means being strong enough to withstand adverse or difficult times. If you base your leadership style on optimism and toughness, you will have a long line of people wanting to be part of your team.*

Regardless of the philosophy that you bring to your leadership style, the important part is that you have a consistent way you show up as a leader. This doesn't mean you don't adjust as needed, are not open to new approaches, or are unable to react to different situations. What it means is that your team understands your underlying style and the way you lead. Whatever your style is now or whatever style you grow into, make sure it is *authentic*.

## WITH LEADERSHIP COMES PRESSURE

"Heavy is the head that wears the crown" refers to the pressure or the responsibility of leadership.

The pressure that comes with leadership may make you feel scared, excited, even indifferent. If you are in the category of being excited by pressure, then you have the makings or already are a leader. It is easy to lead during times of calm. Leading through adversity or through change or rough waters is where we gain our experience and we test our steel.

The areas where you feel pressure as a leader are different for all of us. Some feel the immense pressure of a fast paced, production environment, others feel political pressure, or the pressure of meeting a deadline. Whatever you feel as pressure is where you need to focus your energy to deal with that pressure in a positive fashion. Pressure can be good when we react well or we learn from a reaction that may not have been the best in the moment. Some people thrive under pressure and actually perform at their highest level when under pressure.

## SETBACKS

You will encounter setbacks. We all do. The true test of leadership is how you lead through those setbacks and how you recover after those setbacks. The easy thing to do after an organizational or team setback is to analyze and blame. If this is your style, you will not be seen or respected as a leader. Use those times of setbacks or bumps in the road as opportunities to bring the team together, for everyone to learn—but most importantly, to support those that feel responsible.

Optimism can allow you to overcome setbacks and move forward. This is not always easy, and you cannot have blind optimism. Admit that you or the team has been dealt a bad hand, but you are moving forward as a team.

## VULNERABILITY

### DOUG'S EXPERIENCE

*I recently went through a divorce. That time has held some of the most difficult days of my life. What I was going through impacted my work and my engagement with those I worked with. I was not showing up like I had in the past, and I suspect it will affect the way I show up for the rest of my career and life. Initially, I felt that anything less than showing up as I had the day before my life changed was unacceptable. I learned that, as leaders, we have the responsibility to show others that it is okay to change our leadership presence when we are dealing with other challenges in life. There were those around me at all levels of the organization that offered their support. I used that support. I encourage you to also use the support of friends and colleagues. When they are offering their assistance, they generally mean it and it makes them feel good to help. Everyone has their own level of what they want to share and who they want to share it with. I did share my struggles. I was vulnerable. The result was an amazing amount of support from individuals and the organization.*

## RESILIENCE

Ensuring that you are resilient is critical to how you will show up as a leader. We are not always aware of when our resiliency will be tested so be proactive and mentally and physically prepared for those rough waters. Check in with those around you to get their opinion on where they see your resiliency and if they can offer suggestions or support.

## DOUG'S EXPERIENCE

*On the wall of a gym where I completed my yearly defensive tactics training was the quote: "train hard—fight easy." I try to bring this idea to my leadership everyday—so that when "things get real," I am ready.*

How you show up as a leader will evolve over time as you grow as a person and as an authentic leader. It is a journey. Use every challenging time as an opportunity. Find what fills your gas tank and do it often. If it is reading, then read. If it is exercise, then find time in your schedule to work out. If it is spending time with family, then make it a priority. Ensure you find time in your busy life for self-care to keep your energy levels high for when you need them.

## PEOPLE ARE PAYING ATTENTION

## DOUG'S EXPERIENCE

*I worked for a manager that appeared to be the perfect leader: knowledgeable, articulate, strong and capable. But as I moved up in the organization, I was able to observe this leader in smaller groups and in more intimate settings. His actions and comments were much less "leaderlike" and were in fact embarrassing to me. Now many of us may behave differently at work versus home, but in this case, the leader was behaving with completely different ideals, moral standards, and integrity. This new behaviour really contrasted with how that leader showed up in public and to the larger organization. I lost a great deal of respect for this leader as he obviously had two versions of himself. I was left wondering who the real person was; his duplicity had eroded my trust.*

People in the organization, those who report to you and those who do not, are watching you. They may not say it, but they all have expectations of you as a leader. A career of positive leadership can be eroded quickly when your actions are not congruent with what you speak to your team.

## MAKE DECISIONS AND OWN THEM

A leader will make hundreds of important and impactful decisions during their career. The decisions may not always be the right ones, but an effective leader will stand by their choices.

Never be afraid to have an opinion and make a decision. Never blame others publicly, even when their actions caused significant problems. People are watching you as the leader to see what you do—do you step up and accept the brunt of what is coming at you or do you let the negative consequences fall on your team?

As a leader, it is important for you to own your mistakes, but equally important to celebrate your success and accomplishments. You may not enjoy the limelight and would rather not toot your own horn because it makes you uncomfortable. It is, however, important to self-reflect and gain energy from your success and learnings and to use that energy and knowledge to build and strengthen your resiliency. Whether you are surrounded by others or sitting in quiet reflection on a log in the forest, it is important to say to yourself, "I knocked that one out of the park." We are often our own biggest critics; but we need to dig deep, take credit for our success, and celebrate, as well.

## RUN WITH SCISSORS

As a leader, be excited by pressure, take calculated risks, share, leave no one behind, and be kind throughout the entire show. Enjoy every minute of your leadership journey.

## REFLECTION QUESTIONS

1.  Who is the leader with the most effective presence that I have been exposed to and what made them powerful to me?

2.  How do I show up as a leader?

3.  How do I want to show up as a leader?

4.  What experiences have I had that influence how I show up as a leader?

5.  How will I develop my own resiliency?

6.  What will I do when I feel like I am not capable as a leader?

# Emotional Intelligence

*"It is very important to understand that Emotional Intelligence is not the opposite of Intelligence, it is not the triumph of heart over head. It is the unique intersection of both."*

David Caruso, PhD
Co-author of The Emotionally Intelligent Manager
and Anchors of Emotional Intelligence

Leadership is about people and creating an environment where those people can be engaged and productive. Leadership is an active role; *lead* is a verb. There's no way around this. To be an effective leader you need to be able to understand and influence people. People are complicated and emotional—so as a leader, the better you can understand people, and yourself, the more you can influence your team to achieve excellent results.

If you enter a search into Google to find what the top skills organizations are looking for in today's leaders, you will certainly see Emotional Intelligence or "soft skills" such as interpersonal skills, flexibility, and resiliency, in the Top 10 list. The technical skills that got you promoted into a management position are not the same skills you need to be an effective leader. Emotional Intelligence (EI) plays a major role in your effectiveness in running a successful team.

Emotional Intelligence (EI) is about how you, as the leader, behave and how your behaviour makes those around you feel and perform. There are four EI key areas that are important to the role of a leader.

## SELF-AWARENESS

The first key area in EI is a leader's ability to be self-aware. When you, as the leader, understand your own emotional intelligence and areas of strength and challenges, you can begin to set up goals and strategies to help you develop in these areas. Your professional development should focus on gaining a clearer insight into your leadership style and how you manage your team. If you want to bring out the best in others, you need to be able to bring out the best in you.

An excellent way to increase your self-awareness is to participate in a 360 Assessment. A 360 Assessment is a tool that is used to solicit feedback from the leader's team, colleagues and other relevant staff members about the leader's performance. The tool helps to identify the individual's strengths but also uncovers blind spots the leader may not be aware of in their leadership style. You can then focus your professional development on these key areas to help you grow as a leader. Consider gaining a better understanding of self-awareness by taking a course, reading a book, or working with a coach.

## SELF-MANAGEMENT

The second key area of EI is a leader's ability to self-manage their own emotions. When you are faced with stressful situations in your leadership role, it is important that you are able to manage your emotions. For example, a leader who loses their temper easily and shouts at staff when a mistake is made is probably holding their team back from reaching their full potential. When a leader is self-aware of his or her emotions and has developed tools to self-manage those emotions, they are able to act in a calm manner, typically resulting in positive interactions with their staff. Catching yourself in the moment, stopping, pausing and taking a breath, can change the outcome of the situation. There are many ways that you can de-stress and calm down—such as taking a walk or implementing mindfulness and mental fitness practices into your daily routines.

Imagine a stressful situation at work. Instead of dealing with the stress in a calm, rational manner, your go-to behaviour is to start yelling at your team. The yelling creates an environment where your team worries constantly about making a mistake and they feel they have to walk on eggshells with you. You may have no idea that your behaviour is impacting the team so this pattern continues. Your team may be able to make deadlines and complete the required work, but you wonder why you can't take the team to the next level or why your group has so much turnover and sick leave requests.

## SOCIAL AWARENESS

The third key area of EI is social awareness. Are you able to walk into a room and "read the room?" Are you able to recognize others' emotions and the dynamics at play when you come upon situations?

Empathy is a significant part of social awareness. Daniel Goleman and Paul Ekman identified three types of empathy: cognitive empathy (you know what someone else is feeling), emotional empathy (you feel what someone else is feeling), and compassionate empathy (you are moved to help the other person).

Let's take a look at an example. Imagine you have an employee who has been working hard on a special project. She was excited about the project because it is providing an opportunity for her to learn and grow as well as to demonstrate to senior leadership what she is capable of. She receives news that the project has been cancelled due to budget restraints. You can tell she is devastated by the news.

Your cognitive empathetic response might be "I know this news is upsetting to you."

Your emotional empathetic response might be "I feel terrible that this opportunity has been taken from you."

A compassionate empathetic response might be "Let's do some brainstorming to come up with some other ways you can create opportunities for growth and development."

Joshua Freedman, an expert in EI and CEO of Six Seconds, talked about empathy as an emotional connection. He said you don't give empathy or get it. You co-create a space of connection.

This is how he describes it: "As you start to feel more compassion, openness and vulnerability and you step into the conversation more authentically, the other person will feel it ... then it grows .... you go back and forth to deepen empathy ... as you become more courageous in opening up and being vulnerable, taking risks, the other person will too and you'll expand the space of empathy."

Empathy is about creating connections. As a leader, this is important because when people are disconnected, they're less motivated, less willing to share information and act collaboratively, and they're less likely to stay with an organization or come on board with change.

## RELATIONSHIP MANAGEMENT

The fourth key area of EI is a leader's ability to manage relationships. Human beings are hard-wired for connection. Relationship management focuses on how we interact, coach, mentor and influence those around us. It focuses on how you, as the leader, build relationships within the organization—from the custodial staff to the CEO.

Relationship management has a direct relation to the leader's ability to address and deal with conflict. As a leader, your team is always watching and they are looking to you to deal with conflict.

Leaders need to be able to hold themselves accountable as well as their team members and should not be afraid to have difficult conversations. As the leader, when you let things slide or avoid having those tough conversations, you begin to create disgruntled team members. You may even see the team members begin to operate in silos and or be unwilling to work collaboratively. Unresolved conflict can create a toxic work environment that may encourage office gossip or lead to low morale. If you ignore or avoid conflict, your team begins to break down. Therefore, conflict management is a skill that you need to practice and grow. When you have strong relationships with your team, you can have those tough conversations, which both moves the team forward and builds further trust.

## THE CONNECTION BETWEEN BEING A GREAT LEADER AND EI

Stop for a moment and think about some of the truly great leaders you worked with, those who have impacted you in a positive way. What made these leaders stand out from the rest? What skills or traits did they exhibit that you really valued? Were these skills or traits related to their technical knowledge of the job or were they related to their emotional intelligence and their empathy, compassion, problem solving and assertiveness?

EI is an important commodity within any organization and soft skills built on the foundation of EI is what makes a great and inspirational leader.

### *HEATHER'S EXPERIENCE*

*For me, the leaders who truly inspired me were the ones that had high Emotional Intelligence. In the beginning of my career, I worked with a principal who had an extremely large staff—well over 150 employees (teachers, custodians, secretaries and educational assistants) and what I loved about him was that he would take the time to get to know each and every one of us. The staff loved him and we all felt like valued members of our school community. If we messed up, he was there alongside us mentoring and guiding us. When hard decisions occurred, we trusted that he would make the right decision for the overall organization and we valued and appreciated his leadership. He was flexible and adaptable to change, a great problem solver, and had strong interpersonal connections with the staff. Based on my training in the EI assessment model, EQ-i 2.0®, it would be easy to say that he had a high EI. It showed up in the way he treated staff and students each and every day. It was a sad day when he retired.*

Think about a leader that you did not enjoy working with. What was it that made this working relationship difficult? Was it their technical skills or knowledge about the job or was it more about their EI? When you think about what you would not like to see in a leader, you might say qualities such as: being micromanaged, ruled by fear, no collaboration, not approachable or friendly, arrogant and condescending, lacking people skills, shiny object syndrome and devaluing staff. Many of these answers relate to a leader's lack of EI.

## HEATHER'S EXPERIENCE

*Tom worked for a boss who constantly berated him and the rest of the staff, forming a toxic work environment. Eventually his boss retired, but before doing so, he created a very unhealthy environment and a closed system within the organization. To say he ruled by fear would be an understatement. When I asked my friend why this person was never fired, he said people just accepted his behaviour because he had been with the company for many years and people were too afraid to speak up in case they were fired in retaliation. When he retired, the company hired internally, and his successor continued this pattern of behaviour. At this point, Tom decided that he no longer could tolerate that conduct and left the organization. He shared with me that particular experience has made him a better leader and he promised himself as he began his leadership journey that he would focus on building his leadership skills to support his journey. Today he is an effective leader with a high EI and a staff that loves him. That experience pushed him to envision the leader he wanted to be for his staff.*

## INTELLIGENCE QUOTIENT (IQ) VERSUS EMOTIONAL INTELLIGENCE (EI)

An IQ assessment is a diagnostic tool administered by a psychologist to determine how intelligent someone is. IQ predicts up to 20% success in a job. EI predicts 27-45% success in a job. Your IQ is important but it is your EI that determines how successful you will be in the world of work. Your soft skills are built on the foundation of EI and impact your success as a leader. Individuals with a high EI are typically more successful than someone who just has a high IQ.

Have you ever worked with a leader who was extremely smart and knew the technical aspect of their job extremely well, but was out of touch with their EI skills? Evidence of this may be disgruntled employees who feel devalued or underappreciated, employees eager to leave as soon as the right opportunity to move on arises, or high staff turnover rates. Regardless of IQ or strong technical skills, leaders need to work on developing their EI skills.

## EMOTIONAL INTELLIGENCE AND THE RETURN ON INVESTMENT

Investing in EI has both a direct and indirect financial return. A study conducted by The Institute of Health and Human Potential (IHHP) found that leaders with high EI experience reduced turnover and absenteeism, increased employee engagement, greater sales performance and productivity.

On an individual level, EI will benefit a leader's professional and personal life. EI skills are easily transferable into daily interactions with those around you outside the workplace.

## HOW TO STRENGTHEN YOUR EI

With intention and consistency, EI is something that you can work on and strengthen. Leadership is not a position; it is a state of mind. Creating awareness of your key strengths and opportunities for growth along with designing a strategic plan that will help you sharpen these skills will be beneficial to your leadership journey.

Here are five ways you can begin to strengthen your EI:

**Self-reflect and Journal** – What are you proud of, things you have accomplished in your life, your values and passions, career and life goals? When do you feel happiest and most fulfilled? Self-reflection and journaling are important because they allow us to pause and take the time to clear our mind and to improve focus.

**Manage Stress**

a. Mindfulness – Learn to pay attention to your thoughts, feelings, body sensations without judgement

b. Mental Fitness – Your mind could be your best friend or your worst enemy. Our thoughts, create our feelings and our feelings create action or inaction. Often, when we are faced with challenging situations, our thoughts shift to the fight, flight, or freeze part of our brain. This is where our saboteurs live. These saboteurs can stop us in our tracks and create behaviors that impact how we show up as a leader. In his book, *Positive Intelligence*, Shirzad Chamine shares, "the mind harbors characters that actively sabotage our happiness and success." Mental fitness focuses on teaching us how to shift our thoughts from a negative to a positive response. It allows us to catch ourselves in the moment and learn to quiet the saboteurs through practice and repetition. The more you practice, the quieter the saboteurs become. I like to use this analogy: If you attempt to run a marathon without training it will be challenging. It works the same for mental fitness. If you are not learning to strengthen your mental muscles, it can impact all areas of your life.

c.  Box Breathing (4-square breathing)

Close your eyes. Breathe in through your nose while counting to four slowly. Feel the air enter your lungs.

Hold your breath inside while counting slowly to four. Try not to clamp your mouth or nose shut. Simply avoid inhaling or exhaling for four seconds.

Slowly exhale for 4 seconds. Hold at the bottom for four seconds.

Repeat the box three times. Ideally, repeat for four minutes, or until calm returns.

**Focus on your strengths** – What are you good at? How can you leverage your strengths to help you succeed in your personal and professional life? What strengths can you leverage to make connections with others, manage stress, and make decisions?

**Be vulnerable** – Open up to others to develop trust. Do a 360 Assessment to learn how others perceive you. You can have the best intentions but still not the impact you hope. Do not be afraid to ask for help!

**Find a Coach** – Search for a program that focuses on strengthening specific targeted EI areas that builds in accountability so you can see strengths and areas of challenge.

## ■ REFLECTION QUESTIONS ■

1. What does my gut tell me about my level of EI?

2. What is one thing I could do to increase my EI?

3. How does my EI impact my work environment?

4. When was the last time I got feedback about my leadership? What was my reaction? What did I learn?

5. Of the four EI key areas (self-awareness, self-management, social awareness, relationship management), which one could I explore tomorrow and set specific goals?

**MIND** THE **GAP**

# 6

## Self-Awareness

*"If your emotional abilities aren't in hand, if you don't have self-awareness, if you are not able to manage your distressing emotions, if you can't have empathy or effective relationships, then no matter how smart you are, you are not going to get very far."*

*Daniel Goleman, Author, Emotional Intelligence and Primal Leadership: Unleashing the Power of Emotional Intelligence*

## THE REALITY OF LEADERSHIP IS THAT EVERYONE IS WATCHING YOU.

They're watching what you do and what you say. They're taking note of when those two things—what you do and what you say—don't align. In 2020, in the midst of a pandemic, Prime Minister Trudeau told Canadians to maintain social distancing during the protests following the death of George Floyd in Minneapolis, but then he took a knee among the protestors, clearly closer than the recommended six feet. That contradiction was quickly noted and criticized by the opposition.

Whether or not Trudeau made the right choice is not the point, it simply demonstrates that people are paying attention. You may contend the Prime Minister is a public figure who is covered in the daily media, so of course people are watching. But if you think your employees aren't watching you, then you may not truly be an effective leader.

If your employees are aware of what you do and say, you must be too.

## KERI'S EXPERIENCE

*I've worked with managers who, although they may have had good intentions and really cared, had no awareness about the impact their behaviour and actions had on others.*

*I worked for an Executive who was incredibly proud of her focus on people. My colleagues and I knew that when we were called to a meeting with her, we could expect to set aside an extra 15 minutes to an hour to 'chat'. She felt this small talk was her way of getting to know her employees. To be fair to her, for some employees, it was a great way to build relationships. The problem was, for others, this small talk took time away from work they needed to get done. Her intentions were positive, but the results weren't always. There were also employees who were uncomfortable with the small talk and sometimes even felt it was superficial, not getting to the real heart of any particular matter. Just a necessary evil one had to accept when getting some facetime with this executive.*

*In this particular example, the Executive was unaware that her need and desire to connect with people in a particular way did not match the needs and desires of all those with whom she was trying to connect.*

*In another example, I was the one who lacked self-awareness until it was pointed out to me by my boss. I remember it clearly, despite the fact that it was quite a while ago. She was one of my favourite bosses. I admired her because she was smart, but she also had a high-level of emotional intelligence and knew how to hold people accountable. She was one of those leaders who wasn't afraid to have difficult conversations and managed them with love and grace. That's probably why I recall the discussion and I took her feedback to heart.*

*She told me my facial expressions in meetings made other people feel uncomfortable. Sometimes the look on my face would show disdain or annoyance. I was totally unaware. When she told me, I could not think of an instance when I actually felt the things that were showing up on my face. In my mind, I thought of a recent meeting. I couldn't recall any discussion where I felt annoyed or disagreed with what was being said. What was my face saying to the group? How did this impact the way people saw me? What did they assume was going on in my head? How were my facial expressions making other people feel about me? Was I giving people the wrong impression, a bad impression? I was very concerned when I realized how unaware I had been.*

*Here's another example from my own behaviour. I had an employee who supervised another woman. The woman would come to me for advice. She was young, smart and I felt like I had some wisdom to offer her. One day she came to my office to talk. I loved that anyone on my team felt comfortable talking to me. As a leader, being approachable was very important to me. She looked a little stressed and overwhelmed. She had two young children at home and a husband who wasn't very involved with the work required to take care of the children and household. She was taking classes and was finding it difficult to balance her responsibilities at home, her full-time job, and school.*

*Knowing that I too had a family, a job and had recently completed my master's degree, she came to me to see how I was able to manage it all. In our discussion, I gave her permission to attend to some of her schoolwork during work hours. I suggested that, if she had some downtime at work, she could take the opportunity to get some schoolwork done. She seemed grateful and left my office. I felt good about being able to support her.*

*Her boss, my direct report, came to me frustrated. When she came to my office, she didn't sit down. She was upset with me. She pointed out that this employee (and previous employees) would go "over her head" to get the answers they wanted. In the past, before I became her boss, she had another employee who had a close relationship with the AVP of the division. This employee would go to the AVP when she wasn't happy with an answer she got from the manager. The manager was frustrated and felt undermined. My discussion with her employee was now part of a pattern that wasn't serving her. I had good intentions of supporting an employee on my team. However, because I was not her direct manager, I made some assumptions and decisions that did not align with the manager's expectations.*

*That was hard feedback for me to hear because I thought of myself as a very supportive leader who wanted to set my employees up for success. However, my actions, regardless of good intentions, did not set this woman up for success as a manager. As uncomfortable as it was to receive this feedback, her advice made me a better leader because it increased my self-awareness. I appreciate this manager for being honest and direct with me, even though it was difficult to hear. She pointed out to me something I couldn't see for myself. Because she did, I was able to learn and grow to become a better leader.*

# HOW TO BECOME MORE SELF AWARE

## Educate yourself

There are a multitude of opportunities, formal and informal, to increase your knowledge and self-awareness. If you're not interested in a formal university education, there are courses and workshops offered by many organizations. Still too much for you? Listen to podcasts, read articles or books. There is no end to the tools you can access to enhance your leadership abilities. The more you learn about what effective leadership looks like, the better equipped you are to exhibit those positive leadership behaviours.

## Journal

Taking time to focus and reflect can give you great insight. Have you ever been driving and gone into autopilot, your mind distracted with other things, and suddenly you've arrived at your destination not fully remembering how you got there? You got there because you've made that trip a hundred times. It's a habit and you do it without thinking. There are many things we do without thinking. There are also many things we would do even better if we took the time to think about them.

Journaling gives you an opportunity to think about something you did or said and consider how you might approach it to get better results the next time. Furthermore, if you take time to reflect on a challenge or situation before you speak or act, you could be more effective the first time.

When you journal, consider a particular situation and ask yourself: how could I have handled that better? Think about how you behaved and how others responded to your behaviours. How might the outcomes have been better? How were you feeling in the moment and how did those emotions influence what you did or said? Is this a pattern for you?

## *Self-assess*

There are a number of self-assessments available—personality assessments like Myers Briggs Type Index (MBTI®), Everything DiSC®, Enneagram, and Strength Deployment Inventory 2.0 (SDI 2.0®) or emotional intelligence assessments like EQ-i 2.0®, to name a few. Even if an assessment report doesn't tell you anything new about yourself, it is a reminder of how others might perceive you, which can be helpful. When you read the results of your assessment, consider the impact your preferences have on the way you interact with and lead others. For example, you may be an introvert and your MBTI® assessment confirms it. Being aware of this is just a starting point. You also need to consider how being an introvert impacts your behaviours and, furthermore, how those behaviours could be interpreted by others. As an introvert, you may find social functions draining and so you avoid them. Your team may interpret this negatively and perceive you to be uncaring and uninvested in the group. Social functions can contribute to a team's effectiveness and the individual's sense of belonging. As a leader, you will have to make the effort to participate in these functions. If you behave solely in line with your preferences, you will miss opportunities to be an effective leader.

## *Executive coaching*

An executive coach can also support you to look at yourself and your behaviours and point things out to you that you may not see. A coaching conversation is a safe space for you to talk about and reflect on your behaviours and how they may contribute to your ability to achieve your goals or help you understand what may be holding you back. One of the best things about a coach is they sincerely want to see you succeed.

Education, reflection, self-assessment and coaching are great leadership tools you can use to enhance your leadership abilities. However, the most effective way to become aware of your impact on your employees and peers is to ask them.

## FEEDBACK IS A GIFT

Feedback helps you to learn whether or not your behaviours are having the impact you intend. But, instead of feedback or constructive criticism, consider the idea of "feedforward", a term coined by leadership coach, Marshall Goldsmith, in 2007. It's as simple as shifting your thoughts from what went wrong to what could be better next time. You want to learn from experience. Reframing feedback to feedforward takes away the judgement. You're not saying, "You did a terrible job." You're saying, "You could do even better next time if you changed these things." The focus is not into the past, something you can't change, but into the future, on learning and growth.

Some people may not feel comfortable volunteering feedforward, and often, you'll need to ask for it. You can do this informally, through conversations, or more formally, through peer reviews or 360° surveys. When you ask for feedforward from employees, ask things like, "What's going well?" and "What could be going better?"

Fear can keep managers from conducting 360°s, especially if it might impact their pay or incentives. Asking for feedforward takes courage because it can be uncomfortable for all parties and you may not always like what you hear, but it pays off in at least two ways. First, it gives you an idea where there are opportunities for you to become a more effective leader. Secondly, it tells your employees their input is important, and you want to be a better leader for them, therefore contributing to employee engagement.

One last tip: don't ask anything you don't want to hear the answer to and don't ask about anything you are not willing to change. If you ask for feedforward and do nothing with it, that, in and of itself, is a message to your employees. It tells them you are not willing to change or that their opinion of you doesn't matter.

## ■ REFLECTION QUESTIONS ■

1. What assessments have I done?

2. What did they tell me about myself?

3. What does that mean for my leadership behaviours?

4. What else would I like to know about the impact of my behaviours on my employees?

5. When I ask my employees and colleagues to provide feedforward, what areas do I want to know about?

6. What is holding me back from asking for feedforward?

7. How might feedforward help me become a better leader?

# MIND THE GAP

# Promote Internally or Hire Externally

*"If you are offered a seat on a rocket ship
... don't ask what seat, just get on."*

*Sheryl Sandberg, former Chief Operating Officer, Facebook*

In today's world of employees experiencing a series of positions and careers in a variety of organizations, there is an acceptance of those moving into an organization from outside. It is commonplace and widely accepted.

There are still, however, many organizations that are viewed as more closed due to the culture or unique skills required to do a particular job. This is true in education, law enforcement and other emergency services careers, to name a few.

There are potential landmines to be aware of when advancing from within or joining an organization from the outside for both the individuals being hired and the leaders doing the hiring. This chapter includes strategies that can be used (whether you are the individual who is advancing from the inside or the individual being hired from the outside) to help you be successful in your new role. There are also strategies for leaders deciding whether to advance your staff from within or hire from outside.

# FROM THE OUTSIDE

Leaders who have moved to a new organization are often tempted to quickly make the new organization exactly like their old organization, incorporating wonderful and important changes from their past experience. As a new leader, it is wise to use time as your ally to allow acceptance of you prior to acceptance of your new ideas. Be sensitive to when you may be comparing the new opportunity to your previous post and resist the urge to overuse the "in my last job we" as this may put some people off and detract from the good idea you are bringing forward. This isn't to say one should allow clearly inefficient or inappropriate practices to continue, but a period of acceptance will ensure that your new ideas or ways of doing things will have a much greater chance of cementing acceptance with your team. Your team will need to trust and respect you before they will want to be part of your team or idea.

Avoid comparing your previous organization to the new one. Generally, people are proud of their teams and work units. The constant comparison to others can create fatigue in an organization. Again, this doesn't mean you should not bring new ideas that are tried and true in your previous organization, but do it without fanfare and comparisons between the new and previous organizations.

When joining a new organization as a leader, your primary focus should be to embrace the new environment. Focus on meeting and engaging with those within the new organizations who are respected and trusted leaders. Listen, watch, and seek to understand. Credibility and acceptance will follow.

## BENEFITS AND CHALLENGES FOR THE ORGANIZATION OF HIRING FROM OUTSIDE

One benefit to an organization making the decision to hire externally is the potential to positively change the evolution of an organization when revitalization is needed and there is not the appetite or capacity within to make the changes. This change could be tactical, cultural, or strategic in nature.

There also may be times when a leader from outside has additional skills to take an organization where it needs to go. When recruiting from outside, the organization opens itself up to a larger pool of candidates.

With all benefits, there can also be drawbacks, and the external hiring process can often be longer and more costly, and there is a much greater degree of uncertainty with whom you will bring onto your team.

Don't be too quick to search outside. First ensure that appetite for promotion or hidden talent is not being overlooked. If there are talented candidates not putting themselves forward, analyze why team members are not seeking advancement from within.

## FROM WITHIN

Being promoted from within an organization can be a very difficult transition for some, being "one of the boys or girls" to now being the supervisor or leader within the work unit. Many can transition to this role quite effortlessly, but others struggle in this situation.

It will be important to set boundaries with friends and co-workers while still using your relationships with them to nurture an environment of comfort for ongoing and meaningful dialogue. If you are respected in an organization, then you will be in an enviable position. You will have individuals provide you feedback on how you are performing and what they see as the critical areas the organization needs to focus on. They will also be your greatest allies for reminding you when you deviate from making the best decision for the organization. This is a true gift, so use it to your benefit but never take that privilege for granted.

This transition will often challenge some relationships, so it is critical that you communicate early and often with clear boundaries.

It is common for organizations to promote individuals who are highly effective in their roles to leadership positions. Logically, they want to reward top performers by advancing them. However, many organizations fail to recognize the need to support those people as new leaders. Shifting from the role of "doer" to "leader" can be challenging and the skill set can be very different. For example, imagine a highly skilled surgeon who you might trust with your life. While they may be very experienced and knowledgeable in operating on people, they may not have the emotional intelligence required to lead others—yet they may still be promoted to a position of leadership.

## BENEFITS AND CHALLENGES FOR THE ORGANIZATION OF HIRING FROM WITHIN

As with advancing from the outside, advancing staff from within also has numerous pros and cons of which a leader needs to be cognizant.

You can't buy the significant positive effect on staff morale that occurs when staff see and feel they have a future in the organization. Feelings of belonging and being able to chart a future within an organization will benefit staff retention and tie firmly to career pathing and succession planning from within. In addition, when you hire from within, you have strong and valued knowledge of past work performance. From a staffing and recruiting point of view, when you hire from within, your costs are much lower and your turnaround times are often much quicker.

There are certainly some drawbacks to hiring from within. One is that you will be creating a vacancy which may be challenging to fill. Secondly, those promoted from within can be tested by those they have worked with as peers. Thirdly, not all new leaders have leadership skills. When promoting from within, consider how the organization might support this person to grow their leadership skills through training, mentoring or coaching.

## DOUG'S EXPERIENCE

*I was part of an organization that decided to hire into senior leadership roles from outside rather than promote from within. There were a number of factors considered when this decision was made, including a lack of suitable applicants not wanting to relocate to head office and, quite frankly, a perspective by the senior manager that those "within" may not have the capability to carry out the senior leadership role.*

*After numerous failed attempts with the external hiring of extremely talented individuals with impressive resumes and credentials, a decision was made to hire from within. I was the successful candidate for the position. The result was a feeling of calmness within the organization. The employees felt the new leader (me) understood exactly what their job, challenges and opportunities were all about. It is likely true that I may not have had the qualifications or the impressive resume of external candidates, but I did have the understanding of the many spokes of the wheel of the organization. My growing up within provided those around me a level of comfort to approach me with an issue or provide me feedback they may not have with an external leader. I have received countless calls from staff within my organization who remind me to send out the next newsletter from the boss, or to reach out to a specific employee who is struggling with an issue, or to inform me of an operational issue that had the potential to go in the wrong direction. I value each and every one of those interactions and appreciate staff having the courage to contact me and bring those issues up. This truly is the major benefit of promoting from within.*

## KERI'S EXPERIENCE

*When I was given my first management opportunity, I was promoted to the position of manager of my team. I was the last to join the team and many of my teammates had been with the company for a long time. One had been there more than twenty years. I was the only person internally who had applied for the position. This was an advantage because it meant I wasn't competing with these colleagues.*

*During the time we worked together, I had become close to one of my teammates. We carpooled to work together and, on the drive, shared a great deal about ourselves and our work situations. Once I became the manager, that relationship changed almost instantly. I didn't change the way I spoke to her or behaved around her but when I went from being her colleague to her boss, her guard went up. At the time, I didn't question her. I continued to show her how much I respected her and valued the work she did. We developed a new kind of relationship. While it wasn't the same kind of close collegial friendship we had before, it was still respectful and productive.*

*When you're promoted from within, expect that your relationships will change. However, as a leader, it will be important to nurture these new relationships.*

## ■ REFLECTION QUESTIONS ■

1. If I joined an organization as a leader, how did I feel and how did people behave? What was the impact on me?

2. What are my observations of leaders who come from outside an organization? What did they do well? What could they have done better?

3. What was the most important thing I have learned from someone new to my organization and why was it important to me?

4. What is something I brought to a new job that was not there before I arrived?

5. If I was promoted to a leadership role:

   a. What leadership skills do I need to develop?

   b. What plans could I put in place to support my growth as a leader?

# Work-Life Integration—
# The New Work-Life Balance

*"Don't confuse having a career with having a life."*

*Hillary Clinton*

Work-life balance has been replaced by work-life integration. People are beginning to realize that work-life balance is no longer achievable. The word *balance* refers to something that has equal parts. The word *integration* refers to how all the parts of our life—work, family, health, friends, and leisure—merge together to create harmony.

Work-life integration starts by examining how our core principles and values interconnect or weave together to allow us to live a fulfilling and meaningful life, both personally and professionally. Brené Brown, a research professor and New York Times best-selling author, commented in a radio interview, "The busier we get, the easier it becomes to move away from our true selves." This is particularly true if we are not intentional and mindful of our actions. Staying true to one's values and looking for opportunities to stay true to yourself as you continue on your leadership journey is important. Our values should not be situational, and they should be aligned at work and at home.

## HEATHER'S EXPERIENCE

*When I started out in my career, I was single and spent much of my time, like most of my professional single colleagues, working. I had my first formal leadership role at the age of 30 and was a department head in a high school in Burnaby.*

*I lived in a house just a couple blocks up from Granville Island in Vancouver with three other roommates. Life was pretty good. We had very little responsibilities to anyone but ourselves. We were footloose and fancy free. We worked hard and played hard. Our work-life integration was easy to manage— we went to work and then we played. We trained for running races such as the Vancouver Sun Run and the Ultra Night Run as well as spent time working out at our local gym.*

*As I moved up through my career, I fell in love and got married to my wonderful husband, Derek, and a year later we had a beautiful daughter. My husband's company relocated to Edmonton and so we packed up our things and headed east. After two years in the Edmonton area, we moved to Quebec because my husband's organization's head office relocated to Montreal. It was a challenging move for our family because we are not bilingual. I was able to snag a teaching contract position and worked in Pointe Claire at John Rennie High School filling in for a maternity leave. After a year, we returned to the Edmonton area and I restarted my career.*

*Life was challenging—I enrolled in a new master's program, had a daily two-hour commute, taught full-time and was trying to keep up with all the marking of class assignments—it was crazy! I was juggling my career, being a wife, a mother, and a student—all while looking to move into a leadership position. I worked steadily at this pace for two years. Once I completed my master's, I was on to something else. The word "No" was not in my vocabulary. I remember my parents calling and telling me I should slow down—and I would laugh. My life was definitely **not** balanced.*

*There was a pivotal moment in my life when I knew things needed to change. Life was busier than ever. I was working as a high school administrator, juggling what felt like a million things; I had just enrolled in an executive coaching program through Royal Roads University and worked diligently every evening and weekend to stay on top of my homework. It was a Sunday afternoon and I was dropping my daughter off at a birthday party. As I was leaving the parking lot, another car drove into the parking lot. I had to swerve to the left and ended up driving over a cement block causing the car to come to a dead stop. As a result of the accident, I ended up with whiplash and a concussion, was off work for two months and ended up in physio for two years. The universe was telling me to slow down and I needed to listen.*

*What this situation made me realize was that I was trying to create the perfect work-life balance, but I was putting unrealistic pressures and expectations on myself that I could never be able to meet. Once I came to the realization that having a perfect work-life balance was impossible, I was able to set reasonable expectations and boundaries for myself. Once I came to this realization, there was an actual physical shift that I felt within my body—a sense of relief.*

*My training in* **Positive Intelligence** *(PQ) in 2019-2020 helped me gain clarity and greater insight into why I was living an unrealistic lifestyle by trying to create the perfect work-life balance. I learned that I have a strong hyper-achiever tendency that pushes me to do more and be more and never allows me to take the time to sit in the moment and enjoy my life before pushing onto the next project. This training allowed me to recognize my own saboteur tendencies and how they inhibit me from living my best life. In the* **Positive Intelligence Model***, there are 10 Saboteurs that can self-sabotage our behaviour (Avoider, Controller, Hyper-Achiever, Hyper-Rational, Judge, Pleaser, Restless, Stickler, Victim). Positive Intelligence has taught me to embrace my sage (wise self) and allowed me to integrate the Five Sage Superpowers (Empathy, Explore, Innovate, Activate, Navigate) into my life. By learning to shift my thinking, I could resist pushing myself to have this perfect balance and eliminate my working parent guilt and sense of failure.*

*I still juggle a million things because I am passionate about many things, but I am clear with my boundaries, have a better sense of who I am and how I want to show up in both my professional and personal life. I have learned to protect my yeses with the realization that when I say, "Yes," to one thing, I will have to say "No" to something else.*

## CLEAR VISION, CLEAR GOALS

Work-life integration takes work, and you have to be intentional in how you live your life. It starts with knowing your core values and purpose, and both why and how they align with your professional and personal goals. It becomes easier to protect your "Yes" if you have a clear vision of where you are going. Focus on what you love with your health, career, and relationships. Ask yourself on a regular basis, "Am I doing what I love?" If you answer, "No" to that question, you need to reassess what is going on in your life and adjust accordingly.

Revisit your goals to help you move back into doing what you love.

When you are clear on your career plan and have aligned your goals with actions, it is easier to know what your priorities are and where to focus your energy. Your energy flows to where your attention goes and your energy needs to be focused on your clearly defined leadership goals. Instead of aimlessly moving through your career, have a clear focus as to where you are going and understand what steps you need to take. Opportunities will present themselves to you, and if you are clear about your plan, you will be able to determine which opportunity aligns with your core values and beliefs and career goals. Explore the impact of the opportunity on your professional and personal life to determine if it is worth it or not. For example, you may need to focus a bit more time and energy on your new project but the positive impact moving forward outweighs the short-term effort. Clear goals allow you to create ease and flow in your career and a pathway for you to follow.

What if you have an opportunity to participate in several activities and love them all? You need to revisit your schedule and make sure that you are not committing yourself to too many obligations. Sticking to your schedule can be challenging at times. Use time blocking and a priority system to help stay on track, prioritize weekly, adjust your schedule when things come up unexpectedly, and learn to build in flexibility. Become more comfortable in delegating to others on your team and recognize what you can push back to tomorrow. Using a calendar to block out time keeps you organized. You will be surprised when you set up your calendar and realize how productive you can be while still integrating family time and "me" time. You will learn to be mindful of overcommitting or double booking yourself because your calendar is already blocked out. Using a calendar allows you to see where you are spending your time so you may evaluate whether you are doing so wisely. Find a system that works for you. Check our "Getting Shit Done" chapter for more ideas. Leaders who do not have a system to track and plan may find they struggle with their work-life integration.

## SET BOUNDARIES

Learning to set boundaries is an important aspect of creating a healthy work-life integration. Many new leaders find themselves working long hours. The transition slowly happens over a period of time and the next thing they know they are getting home later and later. They feel exhausted and other areas in life become neglected. Does this sound familiar?

## WHY IS IT IMPORTANT TO BE INTENTIONAL ABOUT YOUR WORK-LIFE INTEGRATION?

Work-life integration is one of the hardest challenges you face as you continue on your leadership journey. You will need to be mindful of how you are spending your time and the areas that you are focusing on. There will be times when you need to put in extra work to meet the demands of the job.

Work-life integration looks different for different people. It also looks different where you are in your career. For example, someone may work 70 hours a week, loves every minute, and spends his or her downtime doing the things he or she loves. They may have a perfect work-life integration for where they are in life. Another individual, who may have a young family, will find it tough working a 70-hour week. It can be hard to make those afternoon school concerts or attend a child's extra-curricular activities, so planning will be key to one's success.

## HEATHER'S EXPERIENCE

*My friend, Laura, a coach, shared with me an analogy regarding work-life integration. Close your eyes, take three slow deep breaths and visualize you are standing outside on the sidewalk juggling balls. Some of the balls are rubber and some are glass. As you juggle, visualize that the rubber balls are your work commitments and the glass balls are your family, friends, and health. If you drop a rubber ball, it will bounce back up because it is rubber. If you drop a glass ball, it could be nicked, chipped, and even shatter. When you drop a glass ball, life will never be the same. Knowing this, how will you begin to prioritize your life commitments?*

*When I first began my teaching career, I worked with a woman who oversaw my department. Her identity was strongly tied to her role as a leader and she had a very authoritarian leadership style. She focused more on her career than on her personal wellness. As a result of her leadership style, she was removed as department head. Another teacher and I found her in the bathroom. She was so distraught we had to call an ambulance. Although the event in the washroom was over 25 years ago, I can remember it clearly. That experience was an important life lesson for not only me but others in the department. We were new into the profession and it taught us that although we love our careers, it is important to focus on our personal wellbeing too.*

*Since I began living my life with more intention and integrating the strategies identified in this chapter, I am living my best life.*

Focus on what is important in all areas of your life. As a leader, when you are intentional about your work-life integration, you gain clarity, confidence, and a clear understanding of where you are heading. The good news is that intentionality allows you to achieve both happiness and success.

## ▦ REFLECTION QUESTIONS ▦

1.  Why is work-life integration important to me?
2.  What can I do to become more clear on my core principles and values?
3.  What can I do to make sure my personal and professional goals align?
4.  What can I do to make my time at work more productive?
5.  At what times in my life did I experience healthy work-life integration?
6.  How would my life improve if I was better able to manage my work-life integration?

# Building Trust

*"Earn trust, earn trust, earn trust. Then you can worry about the rest."*

*Seth Godin, author of Purple Cow, Lynchpin and The Dip*

A leader demonstrates and builds trust with their team in two main ways: by their character and by their competency. In Stephen Covey's book, *The Speed of Trust*, he identifies 13 key behaviours that high trust leaders demonstrate:

- Talk Straight
- Demonstrate Respect
- Create Transparency
- Right Wrongs
- Show Loyalty
- Deliver Results
- Get Better
- Confront Reality
- Clarify Expectations
- Practice Accountability
- Listen First

- Keep Commitments
- Extend Trust

## BEHAVIOUR #1 - TALK STRAIGHT

Leaders need to be clear with their expectations of the team and in the roles of its members. Have you heard the term "straight shooter?" A straight shooter is someone that is not afraid to tell it like it is. They do not try to talk or skirt around an issue or situation; they address it head on. What is great about talking straight is that it allows the team to focus on saying what they mean by being honest and upfront without judgement. The team is not afraid to openly share ideas even if their ideas conflict with other members on the team.

Have you ever sat in a meeting where people do not feel comfortable about sharing their thoughts or ideas because they are afraid of the repercussions? In this type of environment, the culture that has been created is a closed system.

When your leader talks straight, it encourages team members to also do so. When your team feels that they are able to talk straight and share their ideas and opinions openly, you create an open system. An open system gives your team a clear and accurate picture of the organizational goals and the challenges it may be facing. This open communication allows for creativity and innovation to flourish.

## BEHAVIOUR #2 - DEMONSTRATE RESPECT

As a leader, when you genuinely demonstrate that you care for others, they will know. Every member in your organization should be treated with respect and dignity—from your custodial team to your senior management team. All stakeholders are important in the running and functioning of the organization and should be treated with respect. For example, in a school setting, the stakeholders are students, staff, parents, support staff, trustees and members of the senior leadership team. Everyone plays an important role in the success of the school community.

Trust is built by the actions that you demonstrate. Actions speak louder than words. It is by "doing and taking action" that trust is built. Make yourself easily approachable and accessible to your team.

Taking the time to learn about who is on your team shows them that you care.

## BEHAVIOUR #3 - CREATE TRANSPARENCY

Transparency is important in building trusting relationships. Make sure that all of the facts and data are on the table when you are discussing issues with your team.

## HEATHER'S EXPERIENCE

*During the pandemic, as information was shared out through our Central Office, we let our team and stakeholders know what was going on at the school level. We held many impromptu meetings where we not only shared information but were able to address any concerns that our team members may have had. As a team, we would brainstorm ideas/solutions to address concerns and resolve issues quickly. Because our leadership team was transparent, our stakeholders trusted us to help guide and support them through issues that would arise.*

## BEHAVIOUR #4 - RIGHT WRONGS

Your team is watching you. As a leader, there will be times when you screw up or make a mistake. When you make a mistake, it is important for you to own up to it, apologize and make amends. Do not let pride or ego get in your way.

It takes courage to admit you have made a mistake. Do not try to cover it up and hope no one will notice. Address it quickly, make restitution (if possible) and move forward.

## BEHAVIOUR #5 - SHOW LOYALTY

Remember to give credit where credit is due. Acknowledge the work of your team and the effort that they have put into the projects you are working on. Do not take credit for all of the work—it was a team effort.

It is also important to talk about your team as if they were there, in the room, when you share their successes. When you work with your team and downplay their efforts, it can negatively impact trust.

As a leader, there will be times when a team member may

share personal information with you that may be impacting their productivity at work. Make sure you clarify with your employee if they want the information shared with the team or kept confidential. Even though you are the leader, remember, it is not your information to share so you will need to respect the confidentiality of your team members.

## BEHAVIOUR #6 - DELIVER RESULTS

You must be able to prove to your team and organization that you can get results.

As a leader, you will be involved in the goal setting, planning and implementation of projects within your organization. It is through your leadership that the team will deliver its results. Show that you can work with your team to set goals, meet deadlines, and stay within budget. Setting up accountability and tracking systems in order to meet your team's goals keeps everyone on track and trusting you as their leader.

## BEHAVIOUR #7 - GET BETTER

Demonstrate that you are a lifelong learner and that you are willing to invest time, energy and money into your professional development. Stretch yourself so that you are learning new things and are able to see things through a different lens. As Abraham Maslow said, "He that is good with a hammer tends to see everything as a nail." Do not be afraid to stretch yourself.

A coach could help you develop a professional development plan that will allow you to strategically move forward in your career. The plan should allow you to focus on areas of growth as well as utilizing your strengths.

## BEHAVIOUR #8 - CONFRONT REALITY

As a leader you must deal with situations that may make you feel uncomfortable. Lean into these situations and deal with them in a timely manner. Your team is watching and will make judgments based on how you deal with challenging situations. Do not downplay a situation when you need to be direct.

No one wants to work in an environment where there is underlying conflict or dissention. Your team members want to be treated fairly and with respect and if you let things slide and do not address issues of concern, your team may begin to harbor negative feelings towards you and question your leadership.

## BEHAVIOR #9 - CLARIFY EXPECTATIONS

Clear expectations help to build trust because your team knows exactly what you expect from them. Clarifying expectations allows you to define the scope of the job and the amount of time and effort needed to complete the work. If you are not clear, your team won't be clear and will make assumptions regarding what is and isn't expected—which can create miscommunication amongst the team.

### HEATHER'S EXPERIENCE

*When I first began to work in the student services department, I shared the role of inclusive learning facilitator with one other colleague. Our responsibilities were not clearly defined. There were certain roles and responsibilities that needed to be accomplished throughout the year; however, neither of us were assigned specific tasks to complete. We focused on our professional areas of strengths and sometimes other areas did not get the attention needed. In order to make our team more efficient, we realized that we needed to clarify expectations and make us each responsible for certain tasks. By doing this collaboratively, it allowed us to create more accountability within our team, eliminate miscommunication, and build a stronger and more effective team.*

## BEHAVIOUR #10 - PRACTICE ACCOUNTABILITY

Systems are important to the success of any organization. As a leader, you must create systems that will easily hold you and your team accountable in setting and reaching goals. Whether it is weekly team updates or check ins, you need to ensure the team is on track. Make sure that your system results are measurable because what gets measured gets completed.

## BEHAVIOUR #11 - LISTEN FIRST

The golden rule of listening is to listen first to understand not to respond. When we are in conversations, many of us start to formulate our response even before someone finishes speaking. We focus on our own agenda and, unfortunately, do not actively listen to others. Some people will even cut others off before they have finished speaking. A good leader will take the time to be curious, ask questions, and lean into the conversation. A simple phrase, "Tell me more" goes a long way.

## BEHAVIOUR #12 - KEEP COMMITMENTS

As a leader, if you say you are going to do something—do it! Make realistic commitments so they can be completed in a timely fashion. When you make a commitment and constantly break it or blame other people for being the reason you couldn't complete it, eventually you begin to lose credibility. If you struggle to follow through with large commitments, then start small.

## BEHAVIOUR #13 - EXTEND TRUST

Trust builds trust. In your role as a leader, you need to demonstrate to your team that you trust their ability to get the job done. If you assign a specific task to your team, be there to support, if needed, but don't micromanage the project. When you extend trust to your team, you are empowering them. In turn, your team reciprocates the feeling of trust because you believe in them.

Think of a time in your career when someone demonstrated trust in your abilities. When others believe in our ability, we want to do better. A great example of extending trust occurred during the COVID 19 pandemic. With very little warning, many employees had to work from home. Organizations had to extend trust to their staff, believing employees would get their daily work completed. Many employees had to juggle the commitments of work and home at the same time and demonstrate they were able to successfully manage their workload.

Covey wrote, "Extend trust is based on the principles of empowerment, reciprocity, and a fundamental belief that most people are capable of being trusted, want to be trusted, and will run with trust when it is extended to them." When you show that you truly trust someone and believe in them, they will, in turn, have more trust in you.

## BUILDING TRUST AS YOU TRANSITION INTO A NEW TEAM

Building trust in your work environment goes back to two key factors: your personal character and your competency. In your career, you may have the opportunity to work in different leadership settings and various departments. We know that having the title of "leader" does not mean that people will automatically trust you. Your team will need time to get to know you and see you in action. They may follow you in the beginning, but it does not mean that they necessarily trust you. The way you interact with others by demonstrating characteristics such as integrity, fairness, kindness and authenticity along with your ability to lead others and get things done are important in building their trust in you.

Spending time getting to know your staff helps develop trust and it can easily be done by dropping into their work areas, eating lunch in the staff room and participating and being visible in staff social activities. Keeping an open-door policy plus spending time getting to know more about who is on your team will help to build trusting relationships. Also, as you lead projects, your team begins to see you in action and each successful project continues to build trust in you as a leader.

### HEATHER'S EXPERIENCE

*In September 2020, in the midst of the COVID pandemic, I was transferred within my school division to a new leadership team in a new community. Staff and students wore masks and we were following strict guidelines outlined by my school division and Alberta Health Services to ensure everyone's safety. I only knew a handful of staff and a few students in this school community so as I transitioned in, my main focus was on building trusting relationships with the staff, students, and school community. Integrating components of the 13 behaviours Covey identified in his book helped me to begin to build trust within the school community and build strong trusting relationships with my team.*

## WHY TRUST IS SO IMPORTANT FOR LEADERS TO BUILD WITH THEIR REPORTS

As a leader, building trusting relationships is one of the most important things you can do. When you build connections with your team, they feel seen, heard and understood which allows them to feel valued members of the team. When people feel valued on the team, they will work harder to meet their team goals. When employees feel that the leader has trust in their ability, they reciprocate that feeling of trust back to the leader.

Building trust within your team is critical to the success of an organization. A trusting team can result in increased productivity, a greater sense of loyalty to you and the company, decreased sick days and less staff turnover. The leader, like a captain of a ship, is at the helm of their team and is instrumental in the organization reaching its goals.

Growing and nurturing a trusting work environment needs great care and attention. Revisit the systems that you have designed to ensure that they are meeting the needs they were developed for. Include your team leads in the process as well to help address any questions and concerns on your team. Do not wait until tomorrow. Today is a great day to get started.

### ■ REFLECTION QUESTIONS ■

1. What does trust mean to me?

2. Who are the people I really trust and how was that trust built and nurtured?

3. What behaviours do I now have that help build trusting relationships? How are my behaviours reflected in the actions demonstrated by my team and organization?

4. How do I build trust when it has been broken?

5. What are the positive impacts of my direct reports having more trust in me?

# Effective Communication

*"The single biggest problem in communication
is the illusion that it has taken place."*

*George Bernard Shaw, recipient of the Nobel Prize for Literature*

Your ability to communicate effectively is one of the most important skills you will need as a leader. You need to be intentional about when, what and how you communicate.

Many people overestimate their ability to communicate effectively. They don't do it enough or they don't do it well. They assume that if they have the ability to speak or write, they are effective communicators.

When things go wrong, at work or at home, it's often because there has been a problem with communication. Have you ever asked an employee to do something only to find they haven't met your expectations? It's very likely you had those expectations clear in your mind but didn't communicate them clearly to the employee. If you've ever said, "You didn't tell me that," you've been on the receiving end of poor communication.

We are all guilty of ineffective communication. It's nearly impossible to get it right every time. However, there are tools and strategies that can make you more effective.

Consider the idea of "big C" and "little c" communication. In the simplest terms, Big C is about corporate communication, or the things the company shares with its broad audiences (such as the website, annual report, CEO presentation, and marketing materials). Small c refers to the communication between individuals and, most often, it's the kind of communication that happens between a manager and her employees.

# BIG 'C' COMMUNICATIONS – COMMUNICATING WITH A LARGE AUDIENCE

## KNOW YOUR AUDIENCE

You will be more effective at communicating when you understand who you are addressing. Think about:

- What level of information do they need?
- How much detail will they want?
- What kind of terminology are they familiar with (for example, will they know what those acronyms mean)?
- How might they react to your communication?
- What kinds of questions will they have?
- How do they prefer to receive information?

## DEFINE YOUR OBJECTIVE

Before you craft your message, consider what you want your audience to think, feel or DO. Why are you communicating? The clearer you are about what you want the recipient to do with the information you're providing, the clearer your message will be.

## MAKE A PLAN

When you need to communicate, especially when it's about something important, take some time to make a plan. A template is included as an appendix to help you work through all the things to consider when creating a communications plan. If you have access to a communications professional, use them and leverage their expertise.

## KERI'S EXPERIENCE

*Many years ago, I was driving to work, to a job I had held for nearly three years, when I heard on the radio that the company I worked for had been sold. Before that moment, employees were given no indication that this change was under consideration. In fact, in the past, employees had been reassured that a sale wasn't even being contemplated.*

*Instantly I felt betrayed. I was mistrustful of our leadership and I was afraid for my job. These feelings contributed to my behaviors in the coming months. I became disengaged, unconcerned about whether or not my work contributed to the company's success. In speaking with my colleagues, I learned that I wasn't alone.*

*If the company had planned the communication to inform employees in advance, they could have addressed the fears and maintained trust.*

## THE FOUR Cs

When you craft your message, remember the following four Cs.

*Clear* – Make sure your message is clear and leaves no room for misunderstanding. It is helpful to have someone else review your messages before sharing them more broadly. Choose an employee you know would have concerns or questions and ask them for feedback. Don't take it personally, incorporate that into the message.

Use simple language. While you might think using big words makes you look smart, it might contribute to confusion. Simple and clear is best. For example, 'use' and 'utilize' mean the same thing. 'Use' is simpler.

*Concise* – People can only consume so much information before they start to experience cognitive overload, preventing them from hearing, understanding and remembering what you've shared. Try to narrow down to three key messages focusing on what you want people to *feel*, *think* or *do* with the information you're sharing.

*Complete* – When you leave room for interpretation, people will come up with their own interpretation and it might not be what you intended. If there are questions you don't have the answers to or information you don't have yet, it's better to address it straight on and let people know when to expect more information.

*Consistent* – Make sure your communication is consistent with what you've said before and consistent with what your organization is saying overall. You don't want to confuse people.

## COMMUNICATION IS TWO-WAY

There are many types of media for one-way communication but in leadership, communication should always be two-way and rarely, if ever, one-way.

Listening is just as important as talking. People want to be seen, heard and understood, especially in the workplace where they spend the majority of their adult lives. When you understand people by listening to their hopes and fears, ideas and goals, your communication will be more effective.

Let's look at an example. Marilyn is the CEO and is very effective at sharing her vision of the company. She often meets with groups of employees to discuss corporate priorities and describe what she sees for the future. She opens the floor to questions but rarely receives any which she takes as a sign that all is good.

But all is not good. For whatever reason, people don't feel comfortable speaking up in those meetings (this is a problem in itself). Maybe they don't want to appear foolish in front of their colleagues. Perhaps, in the past, people were reprimanded for voicing concerns. Or maybe it's just as simple as people not wanting to speak up in front of a larger group. Whatever the reason, Marilyn is assuming people are satisfied with what they've heard based on the lack of feedback in her group meetings with employees.

Does this scenario sound familiar? The CEO or President makes a presentation and is met with silence. The CEO goes back to her office thinking, *That was great! I did a good job.* Following the meeting, people go back to their smaller work groups and the conversations start. "What does this mean for us?" "Have they considered this?" "What about that?" "That will never work." "Our competitors are going to crush us." It might be days, weeks or even months before concerns are discussed and addressed, if ever. In the meantime, work begins to move forward and the challenges, that might have been pointed out earlier, become roadblocks that slow things down, or worse yet, require a new plan.

Imagine if the meeting went a little differently. Marilyn shares her vision and the corporate priorities in a presentation. Then employees break out into smaller groups of five (a much safer place to speak up). Each group must assign a note-taker and a presenter. The groups are asked to discuss three things:

- How does the work you do align with the vision and priorities?
- What obstacles do you see and how might we overcome them?
- What questions do you have?

The groups come back together and share the results of their small group discussions. Marilyn is able to answer questions. Themes begin to emerge.

The result? Marilyn walks away better equipped to lead and support the company to achieve the vision. Employees walk away feeling their concerns have been heard. They understand what needs to happen and they have a clear line-of-sight from their work to the corporate vision.

This is one example of a way to encourage two-way communication. There are many ways to encourage discussion. It's important to find the ones that work for your organization. Silence is not always golden when it comes to employee communication.

## SMALL 'C' COMMUNICATIONS - COMMUNICATING WITH THE PEOPLE WHO REPORT TO YOU

Many of the rules that apply to big C communication, also apply to the small c communication, which happens between a manager and her employees. In general, employees are more likely to listen to and trust the information shared by their immediate supervisor, especially if there is an abundance of information directed at them. As a leader, you have a responsibility to make sure your employees are informed and engaged so they can be productive and effective in their jobs.

## THE TOUGH STUFF NEEDS FACE-TO-FACE COMMUNICATION

### KERI'S EXPERIENCE

*Many years ago, I was working in what I felt was a great job at an international consulting firm. It was one of my first jobs and I had opportunities to learn and grow, working with a variety of clients. The people I worked with were smart and talented and I loved my boss, Robert. He was a great listener and he challenged me to try new things while also giving me the support I needed to succeed. This was particularly important because I was one of two employees in our communications area.*

*Then one day, out of the blue, I received an email telling me my boss would no longer be my boss. An email. I sat in my cubicle rereading that email wondering if I had misunderstood its contents. I was heartbroken and I felt insignificant, like I wasn't even worthy of a face-to-face conversation.*

Face-to-face communication can be uncomfortable when you have to share bad news but putting these types of messages into an email makes it appear as if you don't have the courage to look someone in the eye. It also removes your ability to support your employees when they react to what you have to tell them. People are complicated and emotional. Leadership requires courage.

## KNOW YOUR EMPLOYEES (YOUR AUDIENCE)

A large part of leadership is trust and one way to develop trust with your employees is to get to know them. Take time to learn about them. Find out about their strengths and where they are seeking opportunities for growth. What are they interested in? Do they have a family? It will also be helpful to learn what they need from a leader. For example, a seasoned professional might want less guidance from you than someone just starting their career, but you won't know this for sure until you ask. When you understand your employees, you can tailor your communication to their style and therefore be more effective.

A note of caution here. Be aware of your employees' boundaries in terms of sharing information and respect those boundaries. For example, in most workplaces, it's not appropriate to share all the gory details about your recent medical procedure nor is it appropriate to ask an employee about theirs.

## UNDERSTAND WHY YOU'RE COMMUNICATING (OBJECTIVE)

There are many reasons you talk to your employees and obviously you're not going to create a communication plan every time you have a conversation. However, it does help to be clear about why you're communicating with them. Perhaps you're sharing your knowledge and experience or training them to do a certain task. Maybe you're just saying good morning to let them know you're in the office and you care about how they start their day. There are times you will be providing feedforward and others where you're learning about what they're working on and how you might be able to support them. There will also be times when you're consulting with them to gather information or ideas. When you and your audience know why you're communicating, your communication will be more effective.

## TWO-WAY IS EVEN MORE IMPORTANT IN SMALL C COMMUNICATIONS

There is rarely a time when communication with the people who report to you should be one-way. Even in the military when a superior gives an order, they want some type of acknowledgement the order has been received and understood. When you're in a leadership position, listening is just as—and often even more—important than speaking. People want to be seen, heard and understood. Theodore Roosevelt, 26th U.S. President, said it best, "People don't care how much you know until they know how much you care." When you communicate something, ask your audience questions to ensure they've understood, then listen carefully to their reactions, questions and concerns.

## CREATE COMMUNICATION OPPORTUNITIES

It's not just about listening when you're face-to-face with your employees, it's also about providing them with opportunities to talk and be heard. The old adage, *no news is good news,* does not apply to your communication with your employees. As a leader, it's your job to provide employees with the opportunity to communicate with you. An open-door policy doesn't cut it.

Here's a simple guideline for how frequently and what you should be communicating with your employees.

***In the moment*** - Provide regular feedback. Don't save your feedback for the formal conversations or, worse, the annual performance review. When you observe the behaviour that needs to be either recognized or corrected, the best time to address it is in the moment, or shortly after (if you need to wait for a private moment, for example).

***Daily*** - Say good morning (afternoon, evening, whatever is relevant). You might not catch everyone, everyday but they'll know you're available. This is also an opportunity for them to connect with you with information or a request.

***Weekly*** - Check in with your employees informally. Ask what they're working on and if they need anything from you.

***Monthly*** - Schedule a 30 to 60-minute one-on-one meeting with each employee. For these meetings you might want to develop a regular agenda. For example:

- What is your employee working on?
- What's going well and what could be going better?
- What can you do better to support them? What do they need from you?

### KERI'S EXPERIENCE

*I was ready for my annual performance review. I had a great year with positive results. I had written a long list of examples on my document demonstrating all the ways I had achieved the goals outlined at the beginning of the year. I wasn't nervous about the meeting with my manager. I knew where I stood. At least I thought I did.*

*Somewhere in the middle of our discussion, my manager brought up an incident that happened several months earlier. He said our EVP wanted to point out that I looked at my phone during a meeting, which she found to be disrespectful. The feedback itself wasn't problematic. I agree that when you're in a meeting with others, they should have your attention, not the device in front of you. In fact, I make it a point to turn my phone over with the sound off so I can give people my full attention. For whatever reason, I broke my own rules that day.*

*The delivery of the feedback was the issue. First, it was delivered by my manager, rather than directly by the person who had the problem with my behaviour. Feedback is most effective when delivered directly. Secondly, it was delivered months after the incident occurred. When that much time has passed, it made the feedback less effective at changing my behaviour and more effective at making me feel like the EVP was keeping a list of my transgressions which would be sprung upon me in my annual performance review.*

As a manager, you're probably very busy, which makes it difficult to find time in your schedule for your people. However, the investment you make in meeting with your employees will pay off far more than any other task on your desk.

To be most effective, leaders must be strong communicators. Whether you're trying to reach an audience of 250,000 employees across the globe or three employees within four walls, you will increase your effectiveness if you take the time to consider your audience. What do you want them to think, feel or do as a result of your communication?

## ■ REFLECTION QUESTIONS ■

1.  When have I been on the receiving end of poor communication? What was the impact on me?

2.  Think of a time you had to communicate something important to your employees. What went well? What would you do differently next time?

3.  Where are there opportunities for me to communicate more effectively with my employees?

4.  What opportunities can I offer my employees to communicate with me?

5.  How can my team be more effective if our communication with each other was improved?

# MIND THE GAP

# Empowering Others

> *"A leader is best when people barely know he exists, when his work is done, his aim fulfilled, they will say: we did it ourselves."*
>
> **Lao Tzu, the first philosopher of Chinese Daoism**

As a leader, empowering others is one of your most important responsibilities. Empowerment is about giving your employees an opportunity to take on a task and providing them with the tools they will need to successfully complete it. It's different from delegating, where you simply assign a task to someone because you already know they have the knowledge and experience to complete it. Delegating is about getting work completed. Empowerment is about developing and engaging your employees.

## WHY EMPOWERING OTHERS IS IMPORTANT

There are two significant reasons to empower others.

The *first* reason relates to employee engagement and development. Think of it from your own personal perspective. Why do you show up to work each day? Sure, there's the paycheque, or the lovely people you get to spend time with throughout your workday, but there's got to be more to keep you interested. That something more is your ability to contribute while also learning and growing.

Can you imagine showing up to work each day and having someone tell you what to do and how to do it, never having the opportunity to grow your knowledge or share your ideas? Would you feel valuable? Would you feel rewarded? People are engaged when they feel heard and have an opportunity to contribute, when they feel empowered to make decisions and when they're learning new things and acquiring new skills.

The *second* reason is slightly selfish and there is absolutely nothing wrong with that. When you, as a leader, empower others to make decisions and take action, it takes the weight off you. It frees up your time. When you don't have employees constantly coming to you asking for approval and answers, you have more time to focus on your own work. It also frees up your mind. If you're not busy solving everyone else's problems, you have the ability to focus on the bigger picture.

## KERI'S EXPERIENCE

*I worked with an executive who was incredibly smart and had a high level of emotional intelligence. She was a loving and devoted wife and mother, an effective manager and strong leader. When she spoke about complex information, she did so in a way that people with little knowledge in the area could understand. She cared about the people who worked for her and would often become emotional when expressing her gratitude to her team. She worked hard and put in extremely long hours. The rare occasion when I would come into the office in the evening, I would often find her car still parked in the lot.*

*I trusted this woman and the advice she gave me about a variety of business and personal topics. I think very highly of her. She once told me about an employee who assured her she had a report that was going to the board of directors well in hand. When the report was presented, one of the board members found an error and the executive was mortified. She felt the error was unacceptable and a reflection of her and the executive management team who reported to the board. When it came to information shared with the board, there was no room for error.*

*After that, the executive had a hard time empowering others. She took a chance and was let down. The result, however, was that she had a significant amount of work on her plate. Thus, the reason for the long hours. Because she was so busy, it was challenging for her team to get time in her calendar. This was even more problematic because the people who reported to her would often defer decisions to her. These were intelligent and highly qualified people who were quite capable of making decisions and taking action, but they were afraid to make a move without the executive's blessing. This often slowed down productivity.*

Empowering others isn't just good for employees, it's also good for you and the organization you work for.

## HOW DOES A GOOD LEADER EMPOWER OTHERS?

### Know your people and their strengths

Empowerment is most effective when you know your employees and what they bring to the table. Understand what they're good at and where they want to grow. Learn about their experience and knowledge. When you know your employees, it's easier to make decisions about what opportunities you will offer them and how you will empower them.

Imagine you have an employee, Sarah, who is your star performer. She's been with the company for several years and brings a positive attitude to the team. Sarah is looking to advance with the company. You know if you don't give her opportunities to grow and learn, she'll eventually leave you to find opportunities elsewhere. You can empower Sarah to start taking on roles and activities that may be beyond her current job. One of Sarah's strengths might be customer service. Because you know she's already good at relationships, you might give her an opportunity to make a pitch to a new client, something she's never done before.

### Equip your employees

Let's continue with the example of Sarah. To empower her (as opposed to just delegating new tasks to her), you'll need to provide her with training, guidance, mentoring, information, or other relevant support to set her up to be successful. When you delegate a task, you choose someone who you know is already capable of completing it. When you empower someone, you give them the opportunity as well as the tools to grow.

In this example, you might sit down with Sarah and go over how you would prepare for the pitch. Then you might have her practice with you before delivering it to the client. Finally, you may go along with Sarah to deliver the pitch. Just remember, you're empowering her so your job will be to sit back and let her do most of the work, but you will be there if she needs you.

## Make it okay for your employees to make mistakes

For people to learn and grow, they have to feel safe to make mistakes. When infants learn to walk, they don't just get up and make their way across the room like a runway model. They crawl first, then they grab onto furniture to stand up and keep their balance. When they finally let go of those supports, they still wobble and fall. Eventually, after much practice, they get stronger and are running so fast, you find it hard to keep up. The whole process might be different for each and every child.

When it comes to empowering employees, we need to be comfortable with mistakes they might make in the learning process. We also have to help them learn from those mistakes. Furthermore, we can provide feedforward, so even if they didn't make a mistake, we can make suggestions for ways they could do even better the next time.

## Know your own boundaries

While it's important to give your employees opportunities to learn and grow by empowering them, it's also important to be clear about your own boundaries. Not everything needs to be a learning opportunity for your team. You have to be comfortable that the work will still get done and the deliverables you need to meet will be achieved. However, if your default is to do everything yourself, you're not behaving like a leader.

## ▨ REFLECTION QUESTIONS ▨

1. What are the skills my employees bring to the team?
2. What opportunities are each of my employees looking for?
3. What opportunities do I have to empower my employees?
4. What support can I provide them?
5. How will I know if/when my employees feel empowered?

# MIND THE GAP

# Recognition

*"We often take for granted the very things that most deserve our gratitude."*

*Cynthia Ozick*

Recognition is critical for a team to function at its full capacity. It is important to individuals and it is important to the team itself. It helps to make people feel valued, and it aids them in feeling that the work they do is seen and is appreciated.

Recognition is often viewed differently by different people. A bonus, a raise, a promotion, or even being named employee of the month are all forms of recognition. These are all obvious expressions of recognition, but there are many other types of recognition, some of them even more meaningful to an employee.

## RECOGNIZE THROUGH ACCOUNTABILITY

When a leader fails to hold staff accountable, others feel they are not being recognized for the good work they are doing. To put it another way, staff feel that they are being recognized when others are held to account for what is expected of them. What a simple yet powerful way to recognize your high performers and your dedicated staff—by holding others to the expectations of their role. Although this may be a difficult expression of recognition to measure, it is a powerful method of recognition for those who are digging in and excelling at their work.

Be careful of *over* recognizing as it can have the effect of diminishing the value of your recognition efforts. When we create an environment where "everyone gets a cookie," we are recognizing mediocrity. This isn't to say that one shouldn't always recognize and appreciate those who show up day in and day out and perform their roles in a satisfactory fashion. There should, however, be some kind of enhanced or higher-level recognition for those who go above and beyond. In its simplest form, there are general employee recognition days, and then there are those special recognition events where a select group of individuals are highlighted for what they do.

## CHOOSE THE LEVEL OF FORMALITY

The type of recognition will depend on many factors, including the type of environment you work in. Some organizations have a formal program, perhaps even with an awards committee made up of a wide variety of staff. They present physical awards, such as medals in shadow boxes, framed certificates and other visual examples of recognition. For other organizations, it is less about a medal in a shadow box, and more about a personal and casual reward such as a gift card. Know your team and your organization and present appropriate recognition for that environment.

## BE TRANSPARENT

There will be times when recognition should be about an individual and other times when the recognition should be about the team. Resist the urge to use recognition as a way of highlighting the organization. Avoid using the act of recognizing someone as a mechanism for another purpose. In other words, be transparent and be true with the intent of the recognition. Although the other goal may be important, the focus of recognition needs to be on the individual or the team that has actually done the work on that project or task.

No matter how hard you try to have a credible and transparent recognition program, you will have hurt feelings. Many people feel they are deserving of whatever award is presented and by presenting it to someone else, you will create the opportunity for people to be disappointed. This situation is normal and individuals need to live with disappointment, but leaders should be aware that this interpretation might occur. The key is that your program is structured and transparent, is awarding recognition for the right reasons, and is fair to all involved.

## BE AWARE OF UNINTENDED CONSEQUENCES

### DOUG'S EXPERIENCE

*Awarding recognition for work or activity that involves a certain behaviour can have unintended consequences. Recently I overheard staff in an organization (that I was not part of) talking about a special recognition award that was presented to a staff member that worked every evening, and every weekend for the last six months to complete a special project. Although the project was extremely important and the employee's efforts were appreciated by the organization, by presenting this recognition they unintentionally communicated to the staff that the only way to receive recognition was to give up time with family on weekends and dedicate it to the organization.*

*Many within the organization shared with me how this demoralized them. In some cases, they were picking up the extra work for the person that was under the spotlight working on the "important project." In other cases, they placed a greater importance on work-life balance, yet still went above and beyond when they were at work.*

The issue is not that the person was recognized, but how they were recognized and for what. Perhaps a quieter and more subtle recognition, specific to that person on the special project, instead a public showing would have avoided the adverse effect on team dynamics. There are those times when extra effort needs to be put in to complete an important project. We all understand that. But you must be careful to avoid the slippery slope where you inadvertently support behaviour that violates your organization's values or good leadership principles.

## ■ REFLECTION QUESTIONS ■

1. Have I ever felt like my work was not valued or appreciated by my boss or organization? What was the impact on me?

2. What has been the most powerful form of recognition I have received in my career? What made this recognition powerful?

3. In what ways can I recognize the accomplishments of my team and individuals?

4. When I reflect on my career, what recognition have I observed that made me raise my eyebrows? What caused that reaction?

# Providing Effective Feedback

**"Feedback is a gift."**

**Author unknown**

Providing feedback to your employees, peers and others around you is a responsibility you have as a leader to help others grow and succeed. This can be simply a conversation with someone where you provide your observations of their actions and engage in a conversation surrounding that observation. The key to effective feedback is that it is timely, meaningful and well-intentioned dialogue which is focused on the individual's success.

Many leaders are caught in the trap of thinking that feedback must be focused on the areas for improvement and the shortfalls of the employee. Nothing could be further from the truth. Feedback is representative of the actions you have observed, both good and bad. The feedback should include both areas of development and areas of success or mastery that can and should be celebrated. Don't feel pressure to balance the feedback for the sake of balancing. If the feedback session is about a specific area that requires improvement, do not water it down with a positive observation if it is not relevant to the discussion.

Providing feedback can be a positive and wonderful experience for both the person giving the feedback and the person receiving the feedback. If you take your feedback sessions seriously as a leader and provide nuggets of gold to those you lead, those employees will remind you of those times you provided that feedback and how it helped their career and possibly their lives. You will have countless examples where you will have observed a shift in an employee's demeanor, approach, work ethic, or other behaviours that is squarely attributable to you having the courage to provide them with needed feedback.

## AN ENCOURAGING CULTURE FOR FEEDBACK

It is important to set the stage within your organization for a culture of feedback. If you are fortunate to be part of an organization that supports and understands effective feedback, then your job may be easier. You will be well served to encourage that feedback culture to continue and to ensure you provide all staff the tools and training they need to continuously improve that culture of feedback.

However, if you are in an organization where the culture is one that either avoids or does not promote feedback, the following sections will assist you in navigating the process of providing feedback.

## WHEN TO GIVE FEEDBACK

If you have been reluctant in the past to provide feedback, challenge yourself to start today. It truly is never too late to start. Start small, have a plan, and follow it. Don't be discouraged. If you are new to an organization or a position, then you are in the enviable position to start fresh and share the gift of feedback.

## DOUG'S EXPERIENCE

*I was on an interview panel to hire individuals into senior leadership roles in a large organization. The competition was held yearly and many of the same people applied each time. They often wanted to be on the eligibility list so they would have an opportunity if a specific geographical location became available.*

*There was an employee that was interviewed yearly who was consistently first* *on the list. He had the correct skills and he aced every interview. However, he was perceived by his team as aloof, arrogant, and off-putting. These were observations that were prevalent throughout his 20-year career. I was not his supervisor, but I **was** the competition chair. During his requested feedback session, I informed him about how well he had done in the interview and asked his permission to provide some additional feedback related to his approach to people. He indicated that I could, and I explained how he was perceived by his team and provided him detailed examples of this. It was as if this individual was hit with a brick. He was devastated that he was perceived this way and he indicated that no one had ever taken the time or had the courage to tell him this. He committed to me that he was going to change his approach to people, check in with his team and further explore with those around him how he was perceived.*

*His team immediately noticed the difference. Five years later, he is a senior leader who is well liked and, more importantly, respected by all those around him. I have found that giving feedback is an art. It has gone from being extremely uncomfortable and stressful for me to something that I now quite enjoy doing. I enjoy it because I owe it to those around me to provide that feedback. I find it rewarding when those receiving the feedback either express to me their appreciation or I see the adjustment in their performance or how they interact with those around them.*

Giving meaningful feedback is not racing at year end to get an assessment signed off so you can tick a box on the form and move on to the next employee. Giving effective feedback is having those important conversations in real time, on an ongoing basis, and with respect for those you are providing it to.

Never rush these sessions and always provide time for a two-way conversation. Ensure the time dedicated to the session is respected and you are prepared, and in a mind space where you can provide the feedback appropriately.

## IS IT THE SAME FOR EVERYONE?

Everyone responds differently to feedback and everyone has their own preferred way of receiving feedback. There will be nuances with each employee. Some will love to have the positive accolades and need it to fill their buckets. Others may want the positive feedback, but quietly and not in front of others. Some don't want positive feedback and are all about hearing only about their growth areas or opportunities to develop. Find a balance that works for you and the person you are providing the feedback to. It is extremely important that you always engage the person you are providing the feedback to as to how the information resonated with them.

## WHY ARE YOU DELIVERING THE FEEDBACK?

A critical piece that requires a gut check every time you provide feedback is, "Am I giving the feedback for the right reasons?" The feedback can never be punitive or vindictive and your intentions need to be true and your actions honourable. If you ever allow personal biases or individual personal feelings to cloud the how or why of your feedback, then you need to re-group and assess how to move forward.

It is truly about building people up, setting them up for success, holding them accountable and walking with them on a path to success.

## TYPES OF FEEDBACK

There are many types of feedback and they all have their own nuances. For example, there is the structured feedback that is provided in a formal setting such as a monthly or quarterly check in. There are the one-off feedback sessions after a project, a presentation or an assignment. The key concepts of all these conversations will be the same.

## BEST PRACTICES

If providing feedback is new to you, take the time to talk with others about their experiences with providing feedback. Have a plan, and simply do it. The anxiety you may feel will slowly leave you and be replaced with confidence. It is vital to set the stage, be fully present, be prepared, and most importantly, communicate effectively. This involves getting your point across, and ensuring that it is understood. The two final but critical steps are to ask the employee their perspective and to agree on next steps.

The setting or location of where you provide feedback can vary depending on the content of the feedback you will be providing. Is it feedback that should be done in private? Or is it feedback that is less significant and can be made in a hallway or in the moment of the task?

Be fully present and engaged with the employee while giving feedback. For more formal feedback, consider turning your chair directly toward them or making a point of turning your phone down or your computer screen off.

If you are dealing with a performance management situation that could lead to discipline, it is critical to engage your labour relations/human resources department to seek their advice and guidance. If you are working in a union environment, always ensure that you are following collective agreements related to process and employee rights. Ensure that you are providing feedback when you have adequate time to provide the feedback and you and the person receiving the feedback are not rushed. Always look inward to determine if you are emotionally prepared to be providing feedback as your emotional state can have a profound effect on how the feedback is given and received. If you are not emotionally prepared, you will not be fully contributing to the potential of the experience.

It is important to always be clear about what you have seen or heard related to the performance issue. In addition, explain the immediate impact of that behaviour and the further effect on the team and organization.

Be very specific when you tell the employee what you would like them to say or do differently, the immediate impact of the new behaviour on their work, the clients, the team and the further positive effect of that new behaviour on their career and on the organization.

## WHAT TO DO IF FEEDBACK GOES WRONG

Be prepared with a plan if the feedback does not go as planned. There is nothing wrong with stopping a session and returning with more information or when you are more prepared to proceed. Always ensure that you are open to feedback. Don't be afraid to ask those you provide feedback to for their thoughts on how the interaction went for them. Be open minded and adjust if needed.

## ENCOUNTERING THOSE THAT ARE NOT SO WILLING TO POSITIVELY RECEIVE THE FEEDBACK

At the end of the day, you are responsible as a supervisor, manager or leader to provide feedback. You are not, however responsible for how the person receiving the feedback reacts to that feedback. In your role as supervisor, it is critical to follow up to ensure steps have been taken toward growth and improvement.

Have no illusion that every session of feedback will be a wonderful and positive experience for you and the person you are providing the feedback to—it will not. It will, however, build your reputation and skills as a leader and give someone the gift of feedback for use in their growth.

How feedback is received is often one of the most accurate predictors of how an employee will perform in the future. Employees who have a desire to receive feedback and improve themselves with self-reflection are key to your organization's success.

There will also be those that you provide feedback to that appear to be listening, responding and engaged, but their later actions indicate that they were not truly listening to the feedback, or they have listened to the feedback, but have chosen to ignore it. Generally, these are the people that have a difficult time self-reflecting. It can be helpful to have them tell you what the feedback truly means to them. Don't be afraid to push them or challenge them to provide their thoughts or comments. This will help to ensure that they have not only listened and responded, but truly heard.

## ARE YOU READY FOR YOUR OWN FEEDBACK?

Fair or not, it is a reality that leaders are observed and judged by those whom they lead. If you are not able to receive feedback or, equally important, you are perceived as someone who cannot receive feedback in a positive fashion, then you will not reach your full potential as a leader. Set an example and show others your willingness to receive and learn from feedback.

## RESPECT

You will gain a massive amount of respect if you are the leader that provides feedback in a timely, appropriate, detailed, and meaningful way.

### DOUG'S EXPERIENCE

*I have had many supervisors over the years and the ones I respect the most are not the ones I necessarily liked the most but the ones that challenged me, providing me with timely and honest feedback. They were the leaders that set me on a path to becoming a progressive leader because of their feedback.*

## ▓ REFLECTION QUESTIONS ▓

1.   Why do I think feedback is important to give and to receive?

2.   What do I enjoy about giving or receiving feedback?

3.   What are the areas of giving or receiving feedback that I find less enjoyable?

4.   What types of feedback have resonated with me previously and what made them impactful?

5.   How do I prefer to receive feedback?

6.   How will I learn how my employees prefer to receive feedback?

7.   What are some areas where I would like feedback?

# MIND THE GAP

# Dealing with Difficult People

**"Difficult people are the greatest teachers"**

*Pema Chodron, Buddhist teacher, author and nun*

Have you ever had a knot in the pit of your stomach and not wanted to go to work because you had to deal with a person who was just simply "difficult?" Many of us have.

## WHAT MAKES SOMEONE DIFFICULT?

The term *difficult people* is very subjective. We are not talking about when we have a personality clash with someone: where how they do the work is different than how we would do the work, or how they speak is too fast or slow, or that they think in a spiral fashion instead of getting to the point. We are speaking about individuals with traits that make them simply not enjoyable to be around. The following are some of the more obvious types of difficult people you may have the opportunity to work with:

## The Chameleon

This individual has one personality with one group and a very different personality and approach with other groups. You have a hard time figuring out which personality or approach will show up.

## The Dictator

This person feels the need to be constantly dictating how a situation will play out. They are not able to work collaboratively but always have to be telling others exactly how things will go.

## The Submissive Team Member

This person often has some wonderful ideas but is never able to provide an opinion. On the odd occasion when they do provide an opinion, they are easily swayed if there is any question or push back to their idea.

## The Contrarian

No matter what the topic or what the issue at hand is, this person is always quick to find someone to argue with. Regardless of the thought or logic put into an idea, this person feels the need to have a dissenting view on the topic.

## The Constant Complainer

This person always struggles to see the bright side, the positive or the opportunity in the situation. They always seem to find the piece of the topic that they can complain about or criticize.

Do any of those sound familiar to you?

# WHAT IS THE EFFECT ON YOU?

There are the obvious effects that dealing with a difficult person can have on you. Then there are the less obvious effects that can affect your work and how you are seen by others. The more obvious effects include feelings of not enjoying going to work as much as you did prior to dealing with this person. Some of the less obvious effects can be the slow chipping away of your normal positive outlook on situations. There is also the risk that you begin to take on some of the traits of that difficult person, or perhaps, in extreme circumstances, you begin to experience medical issues that can be attributed to anxiety surrounding your dealings with that person.

By leaving a situation with a difficult person unresolved, you often chip away at your own positive outlook because you recognize you have not fully completed your job as a leader

## WHAT IS THE EFFECT ON THE DIFFICULT PERSON?

### DOUG'S EXPERIENCE

*I once worked with a fellow who was always happy, engaged, respectful of those around him, and generally a pleasure to be around. That changed over time and he became quite disengaged and toxic to the work environment. I was able to remain unhurt by his behaviour and decided to take the approach of talking directly with him in private about this change. He indicated that his partner had left him and he was battling significant financial challenges. He simply didn't realize he was being difficult. He was appreciative of the discussion and ensured me the negative behaviour would be transformed to something more positive. Over time, he returned to his original self.*

You can never go wrong treating people, however difficult they may seem, with respect and dignity. There are those difficult people who are just always difficult, who simply don't seem to care and are not fazed by the effect of their behaviour on those around them. However, as difficult as you may find this person, stop and think about the effect of their actions on themselves. In essence, try and walk a mile in that person's shoes.

## HOW TO DEAL WITH THE DIFFICULT PERSON

You have three options when encountering a difficult person. You can:

1. leave it alone and live with the status quo,
2. change something you are doing or your engagement with the person, or
3. address the negative behaviour with the person you are finding difficult.

If you decide on the status quo, make sure you are choosing that option for the right reason. Are you choosing that option because, after you have analyzed the situation, you have determined that their behaviour isn't really that big of a deal? If that is your reason for dealing with it this way, then all the power to you and you will be stronger by your analysis. On the other hand, if you are choosing the status quo because you don't want to adjust your own behaviour, or there is a reluctance on your part to address the situation with the difficult person, then you need to further examine your decision.

Changing our own behaviour is not a weakness and it is not giving in to the difficult person. Perhaps you have carefully studied the situation and have decided that there are some tweaks you can make to your own behaviour that will improve the state of affairs. Maybe you have realized that you were, in fact, triggering some of the other person's behaviour. This certainly doesn't take someone off the hook and relieve them of the responsibility of controlling their own actions, but maybe, just maybe, you partially contributed to those actions.

The option that can be the most tough is engaging with the dreaded difficult person. First, ask yourself if it is your place, position or responsibility to bring this behaviour to the attention of this person—or is it someone else's such as their boss? If this is a peer you have to work with, you may decide that a supervisor does not need to be involved. Secondly, if you are the right person, how do you bring it up? How do you approach it?

Timing is everything. A critical tip is to engage in this dialogue when things are going well. Don't wait until that difficult trait or action has just happened. Chances are they are operating at an increased level of stress, as are you. Go back to respect and dignity. Find the right location to bring it up, not beside the water cooler with a room full of people. Appeal to the difficult person's emotions by describing how their behaviour is making you feel. Be open to the response they may have to your communication. There is a chance that there is something you have done or said that has contributed and you were not aware of it until you had this discussion. Try to approach this discussion as a two-way conversation, not a sharp accusation. Thank the person for allowing you to speak about how you are feeling and the effect of their behaviour on you.

## WHEN OPTION 3 JUST DOESN'T WORK

### DOUG'S EXPERIENCE

*My style when dealing with difficult people is to be firm and fair, to be direct but respectful and to do my very best to resolve the conflict in a fashion where both parties can feel good about how things ended up. I recently have been dealing with a person in an organization that provides support to the organization that I am part of. The person is extremely diligent and is quite structured in everything that he does. However, he is guided by policies that are ambiguous and create confusion around roles and responsibilities. The result can often be a misunderstanding about who is ultimately accountable. My initial perception was that this person lacked confidence in decision making so he clung to a policy that lacked teeth to make the work that it referred to meaningful.*

*I tried to work with this person to understand his challenges and the why behind what he was doing. Finally, I recognized that the relationship was not improving, the process was not improving, and the result was going to be widespread and negative. I had a very direct conversation with this person and opened up to him about how our interactions were making me feel. I discussed the impacts to the organization as well, but I primarily wanted to express my feelings of discomfort. I explained that I wanted to work together and come to a solution that would work for everyone. I wanted to do everything in my power to understand his challenges, his reasons, his why.*

*Even after this open and frank discussion, the relationship and process we agreed we wanted to improve did not improve—and actually degraded further. At one point, the individual I was working with actually became threatening and appeared to have lost all interest in resolving the situation we were attempting to work through. I was forced to elevate this issue to an appropriate level where the matter was dealt with swiftly and resolved. I would later find out that my organization was not the only one that was encountering major issues with this person. He was having an enormous effect in numerous areas, across many organizations—and not in a good way.*

The point of this story is that, even after many attempts in dealing with a difficult person, you may find yourself in a position where you need to elevate the matter. Don't immediately jump to this step. Make every attempt to ensure the person you are having issues with feels they have been seen, heard and understood. Also ensure that you too are being seen, heard and understood. Make every attempt to listen carefully to ensure you truly understand the person with whom you are having issues. This may mean summarizing what they have said back to them to confirm you have the same understanding and asking several questions to ensure you are not making assumptions. It's equally important to ensure you too are being clear and understood. This could be accomplished by having them summarize their understanding of what you have said back to you.

## DON'T BE THAT PERSON

However you deal with the situation, deal with it. Don't be that person that is still complaining about John or Betty for something they have been doing since 1990 and you have not accepted it, changed what you are doing, or confronted them. If you have made the decision to accept it, then stop complaining about it to others around you as you risk becoming a "difficult person" yourself.

## LEARN AND SHARE

Whether it is dealing with a difficult person or addressing another issue, learn from it. Put it in your leadership knowledge bank of experiences you have grown from. Use these experiences you encounter to be a better leader, supervisor, and peer. Share your learnings—not specifically regarding individuals—but the concepts you have learned. Share them with other current and future leaders to put more tools in their tool kits as well.

## ▚ REFLECTION QUESTIONS ▚

1. Who was the most difficult person I ever worked with and why did I find them to be difficult?

2. What did I learn from that interaction and how has it made me a better leader?

3. What surprised you about the outcome when you dealt with a difficult person?

4. Have you ever delayed dealing with a difficult person? If so, why? What were the consequences?

5. Are you currently avoiding a difficult conversation? What could be gained if you had that conversation?

# MIND THE GAP

# Managing Difficult Conversations

*"When we avoid difficult conversations,
we trade short term discomfort for long term dysfunction."*

*Peter Bromberg, Library Consultant*

Have you ever worked in a company or team with a conflict averse culture? On the surface, this might seem great. A place where everyone is nice and no one wants to hurt each other's feelings sounds like a very pleasant and respectful environment. However, there are many unintended, negative consequences of avoiding difficult conversations. As a leader, it's your job to hold people accountable and sometimes that means having difficult conversations. Here are some examples of what can happen when leaders don't have the courage, skill, or willingness to have tough discussions.

An employee dresses inappropriately for the specific work environment. Her male boss finds it very uncomfortable to tell her the wardrobe choices she is making are not suitable. As a result, others, such as clients and colleagues, have a negative perception of her based on her clothing choices. She may miss out on opportunities, which could have a negative impact on her career.

A senior leader in the organization has been underperforming. His colleagues and direct reports have been picking up the slack for months. His boss tries to broach the subject with him, but he provides a long list of things on his plate and she quickly lets the subject drop. His reputation in the organization is deteriorating and people are growing more and more frustrated with taking on his work. They're also losing trust in her and her ability to hold him accountable.

In these examples, you can see how avoiding an uncomfortable conversation can have consequences for the employee and the leader. In the second example, those negative consequences go beyond the employee and boss and filter into the organization.

This is when avoiding a difficult conversation can damage your organizational culture. While you may believe you're supporting a culture of kindness and respect, you may actually be contributing to a culture where people are not held accountable, leading to a lack of trust. When you avoid difficult conversations, you contribute negatively to your corporate culture because you are accepting poor behaviour or performance. This can be extremely frustrating to your high performers who may have to pick up the slack. You're also missing out on fulfilling your potential as an organization. When you have uncomfortable conversations rather than avoiding them, you create a culture where people can be open and honest. When people can be open and honest, problems are addressed more quickly, and you can focus on the business. Beyond that, people will feel safer to share their perspectives and ideas, contributing to your company's success.

## HAVE THE RIGHT MINDSET

The first thing to do when approaching a difficult conversation is to reframe the conversation. Rather than tell yourself, "Ugh, I need to have an awkward conversation with Joe."

Tell yourself, "Joe is important to me and, as his leader, I want him to be successful. I need to share my observations so he can grow."

Mindset is half the battle and can have a significant impact on what you say and how you say it.

There's also the idea of feedforward instead of feedback. The general idea is that you're providing information to your employee that will help them move forward. You can't change the past, but you can learn from it.

## PREPARATION AND PRACTICE

How often do we say something in the moment we wish we could take back? The best way to avoid that is to prepare. Here are some questions that might help you think through the conversation:

- Why are you having the discussion with the person?
- How do you want the person to feel?
- What do you want the person to think when you're done with the conversation?
- What do you want the other person to do as a result of your discussion?
- What is the most important thing you want this person to know when the conversation is over?

You have a positive mindset, you've prepared what you want to say, you're ready to deliver. However, for the best results, there's a little more to consider, like place and time.

## WHERE AND WHEN

There are likely many places to have a conversation, but only a very few are appropriate for a difficult conversation. First and foremost, whenever possible, these conversations should occur face-to-face. Second, they should be private where others won't be able to see or overhear the conversation. Finally, consider finding neutral ground. Unless it's a regular occurrence for all employees, getting called to the boss's office can set the tone before your discussion has even started.

When to have the conversation is also important to consider. In general, try to have them as soon as possible. Do not save them for the annual performance review. There's nothing worse than going into an annual review and getting blindsided by something you did or said over a month ago. Additionally, if the topic is sensitive or may have an impact on the employee or their job, the sooner it is addressed, the better. Nobody wants to feel like they've been kept in the dark. Some managers feel like they have to have all the answers before sharing sensitive information. However, the longer you wait, the less opportunity employees may have to ask questions or provide input, resulting in feelings of frustration.

Before having a difficult conversation, put yourself in the shoes of your employee. Consider what they might have on their plate. For example, if an employee is rushing to meet a deadline, perhaps it's not the best time to discuss this issue. Make sure you have sufficient time to spend with the employee to answer questions or manage emotional reactions. Try not to drop a bomb and run off to the next meeting.

It never hurts to practice the conversation with someone else and get some feedback in advance. You'll be better prepared to have the conversation for real. Just make sure it's someone you can trust to keep the topic confidential.

## HAVE THE CONVERSATION

Some people think effective communication is all about talking. It's not. It's mostly about listening. While you have something you need to tell the other person, this is a conversation, not a lecture. People just want to be heard and understood and there may be circumstances you're not aware of. They might have a reasonable explanation for a particular behaviour or situation. Let's look at the first example and imagine things could go two different ways.

### With one-sided communication:

The boss and employee arrange a convenient time to meet and the location is private. The boss explains to the employee her clothing is not portraying her as the serious professional she is and it's damaging her reputation and potential for advancement. What didn't come up in this one-sided exchange is that the employee has been supporting her two elderly parents and her budget has been stretched pretty thin. While she'd love to have a better wardrobe, it hasn't been attainable. She leaves the conversation feeling bad about herself and worried about what to do.

*With two-way communication:*

The boss and employee arrange a convenient time to meet and the location is private. The boss explains to the employee her clothing is not portraying her as the serious professional she is and it's damaging her reputation and potential for advancement. He then goes on to ask her why she chooses to dress the way she does. This begins a conversation, and the manager has an opportunity to coach the employee and find a solution. The solution may not be a better wardrobe. It may be a better understanding of each other and more trust. It might be the manager's attitude that changes and not the employee's choice of clothing.

The employee leaves the conversation feeling supported and understood.

## FOLLOW-UP

One conversation doesn't always result in the outcome you want. Sometimes it takes many. In fact, supporting your employees to improve and grow should be an ongoing process. It may require setting goals and checking in regularly to inquire about progress towards those goals. Change can be difficult, and you can't always expect it to happen after one conversation. The good news is, once you've had the difficult conversation, the cards are on the table, so to speak. You've made it clear to your employee what needs to change and can work together to make that happen.

## ■ REFLECTION QUESTIONS ■

1.  What difficult conversations have I been avoiding?

2.  What do I wish my previous bosses would have told me earlier in my career that would have helped me to be more successful?

3.  How can I improve my workplace and my team if I have the courage to have difficult conversations?

4.  What are the consequences of continuing to avoid difficult conversations?

5.  How can I prepare for a difficult conversation?

# MIND THE GAP

# Coaching your Employees

*"I never cease to be amazed at the power of the coaching process to draw out the skills or talent that was previously hidden within an individual, and which invariably finds a way to solve a problem previously thought unsolvable."*

*John Russell, Managing Director, Harley-Davidson Europe Ltd.*

## WHAT IS COACHING?

Coaching is asking questions to allow someone else to reflect on something and come up with their own plan.

## COACHING FACILITATES GROWTH

Imagine an employee comes to you with a challenge. There are several ways you can approach this. One way is to tell them to figure it out on their own and kick them out of your office. Obviously, this is not great leadership. Another way is to tell them what to do. That might work but the result is that they've not become any more effective at solving problems and they'll come to you the next time they have a problem…and the next…and the next. A more effective way to approach the employee is to coach them. Through this process, the employee learns and grows. They determine how to address the challenge. The result is they have more confidence the next time they encounter a challenge. Not to mention, you have encouraged a more effective employee who won't take up so much of your time.

## HOW DO YOU COACH AN EMPLOYEE?

You may be wondering what kinds of questions you should ask when coaching your employees. There is no magic bullet, that provocative question that will unlock another person's greatness. The truth is it doesn't have to be a perfect question. It's really more about being present in the moment and providing the other person with a safe space to process.

Start by removing all distractions. Turn your phone on do-not-disturb, take your eyes off your computer screen or anything in front of you that will take your attention away from your employee. Turn your body to face them and make eye contact. It can be helpful to find a neutral meeting place where there are no distractions. Show your employee he is your top priority in that moment.

Let your employee drive the conversation. There are a number of questions you can use to facilitate this:

- What's on your mind?
- Tell me about the challenge/opportunity you're facing?
- When we're done with our conversation, what do you want to walk away with?

Help them to look at the situation from a number of angles.

- What have you tried so far and what were the results?
- What are your options?
- What does your head tell you?
- What does your gut tell you?
- What might be the consequences of your choice/action?

The questions are limitless. The key, however, is to give the employee the chance to reflect on the problem (or opportunity). The best thing you can do is be quiet. When there's a lull in the conversation, our instinct is to jump in and fill the void. Resist. It's not easy. It's awkward and uncomfortable. However, silence gives the employee space to think.

Greek coach and psychotherapist, Olga Papatriantafillou, offers these ideas about the benefit of silence in the coaching process:

*The caring silence:* This silence provides a safe place where the employee can grow and open up. It conveys empathy, respect, listening and support.

*The busy silence:* This gives the employee time to process information, form a new idea, or reflect. For example, a question like "What is perfect about this situation?" might be met with silence.

*The mindful silence:* The employee becomes an observer of what they're feeling, of the thoughts crossing their mind.

*The magic silence:* This is the silence before the "aha" moment. (This is the moment when coaching feels so rewarding because the coach can actually sense a shift in the employee as they start to see the possibilities.)

You will want to fill that silence, but be patient.

Once you've given your employee the chance to think through something, prompt their learning or insight by asking:

- What's become clearer to you?
- What opportunities do you see now?
- What have you learned?

Finally, don't let them leave without a plan. Ask them about their next steps, their own deadlines and what might get in their way. Ask them how they will hold themselves accountable.

Keep in mind, while you may have a great solution to the challenge your employee is facing, giving them the answer doesn't give them the opportunity to develop their own problem-solving muscles. You might learn something in the process too.

## ▨ REFLECTION QUESTIONS ▨

1.  When my employees come to me with challenges, how can I help them to find their own solutions rather than providing them?

2.  As a leader, do I feel as though I need to have all the answers and if so, what is the impact on my employees?

3.  What might be gained if I use silence as a tool?

4.  How will I incorporate coaching into my conversations with employees?

# When and How to Let Someone Go

*"Dealing with employee issues can be difficult but not dealing with them can be worse."*

*Paul Foster, CEO The Business Therapist*

True leaders care about people and they ensure the people they lead are treated fairly and with respect. However, there will be times in your career as a leader and a supervisor when you will encounter employees that are not a fit for the role they have in your organization. There can be many reasons for this.

You may deal with staffing matters that involve illegal activity, serious breaches of policy or inappropriate behaviour. You may also encounter examples where staff simply do not have the skills to carry out the role they are in and your assessment is they will not evolve to where they need to be. Once all attempts and all appropriate resources have been applied to correct a situation and you are not seeing the movement that you need, you may have to make that decision to let someone go from the organization.

The consequences of allowing a negative relationship between an organization and an employee to continue can be widespread. Many of the impacts are difficult to measure but can be devastating to an organization. In many workplaces employees that are affected by another employee's behaviour will often speak of the situation to their peers but will resist bringing it up with their supervisor. The failure of the organization or the leader to take appropriate action can result in staff turnover, increased absenteeism, illness, and lack of productivity.

## DOUG'S EXPERIENCE

*I was once involved in the termination of an employee from his position as a middle manager. The decision had nothing to do with his work ethic. In fact, he was quite far ahead of others in that regard. He also had the ability to manage a great deal of complex work tasks. This individual was one of the highest performers.*

*The issue was clearly his impact on the team dynamic and morale, as well as how he dealt with key partners from other organizations. The feedback from partners and peers was that this employee was simply toxic to positive relationships. That spoke volumes to me about the impact one person can have, not only on their own organization, but to customers, stakeholders, and other partners. We provided the individual all the support that was reasonable and fair to help him grow to be successful, but in the end, he was not moving towards the behavioral change needed and he was let go.*

*The effect was immediate, and the entire team dynamic changed. People once again felt free to speak. Trust began to return within the team, and a collective and collaborative mindset returned.*

## HOW TO LET SOMEONE GO

There are simply those that are not a fit for the role they are currently in and it is best for them and the organization to part ways. Some will recognize this and will willingly move on. Regardless of what collective agreements or company policies exist, ensure that you look after the person being let go, ensuring they have access to appropriate support. That person will remember how they were treated during those final moments and that is extremely important to how they will recover from the events of what has just occurred. It is important to ensure that you do not use trigger words such as 'incompetent' or 'untrustworthy' and are sensitive to the situation at hand. You will be judged by the amount of respect you show and the dignity you afford the exiting employee.

## DON'T TAKE IT PERSONALLY

Remember these are highly charged situations and the employee being let go is processing many emotions. They may say and do things in the heat of the moment that will be difficult for you to not take personally. At the time of the termination, the employee may feel hopeless and angry. Depending on your policy around the termination, there may be a second person providing support in the room. The role of this person is to help the employee navigate what is happening and inform them of the supports that are available to them as they move forward. Some employers allow or permit the employee to bring their own support person into the room. (This can have a positive or a negative outcome. There are truly so many variables and no situation is exactly the same.)

It is critical to look after yourself when dealing with matters like this. This will take a toll on you emotionally and you need to be vigilant in gauging the effect it has on you. Do not hesitate to reach out and get the help you need when dealing with complex matters such as these, especially if you deal with these types of situations on an ongoing basis.

Although you never want to allow letting someone go affect you personally, you also never want to develop a coldness to the situation. There is a marked difference between toughness to get the job at hand done in a respectful and professional fashion and coldness or indifference.

## WHAT WILL THE DAY LOOK LIKE?

Engage your human resources department early and pay close attention to their advice. When it comes time to deliver the termination, you will need to ensure you show up with compassion and respect, but also confidence, toughness, and control of the situation. It is no longer the time to debate the situation at hand but to deliver the termination and transfer the employee to the support services you have available for them.

## HOW WILL THEY REACT?

Every situation is different and unique as no two people are the same. It helps to have a solid plan and a general sense of how you will respond to their reaction. There have been situations and actions that have been tragic as a result of dismissals. It is also extremely important that the dignity of the person being dismissed is upheld throughout, as it will help to ensure that the reaction you receive is as calm as possible. Although it is important to show empathy and allow a degree of time for the dismissed employee to react, it is important that you are always in control of the situation and do not enter down a 'rabbit hole' of defending or debating the decision for termination, as they can inflame the situation. Always prepare for the worst, but expect the best in these situations.

## MANY ARE WATCHING

You will be surprised as to the number of people silently sitting on the sidelines watching the situation play out. They will be judging you by how you handle matters such as this. By dealing appropriately with low-performers or people who don't demonstrate positive workplace behaviour, you are rewarding the employees who are working hard in a productive and positive fashion. You are sending a message to all the other employees that bad behaviour is not tolerated and that you don't expect them to carry the load of under-performing employees.

## ▓ REFLECTION QUESTIONS ▓

1. If you have been in a situation that required you to dismiss an employee, how did you feel leading up to the event? (If you have not been in this situation before, how do you think you would feel?)

2. How did you feel after the event? (If you have not been in the situation, how do you think you would feel?)

3. If you were the person being dismissed, what are three things that would be the most important to you at the time?

4. What can you do to ensure you are well after a situation like this?

## Systems Thinking

*"Nothing ever exists entirely alone; everything is in relation to everything else."*

*The Buddha, founder of Buddhism*

To be an effective leader, it is vital to understand the context in which you are leading. Systems thinking is about analyzing behaviours and events within that context. In an organization, that context might include the corporate culture and values, the organizational structure, how individuals think based on their knowledge and experience (mental models), and really anything that might influence what, when, where, how and why events occur. To look at a system, identify the parts that interact and produce an outcome.

It's helpful to draw the system, creating a system map. Let's look at an example: ABC Company is a system. Within that system there is a corporate structure and perhaps various levels of hierarchy (to keep things simple for this example, let's assume there are two levels: management and non-management). There may be silos within the organization, for example, research and development and sales and marketing.

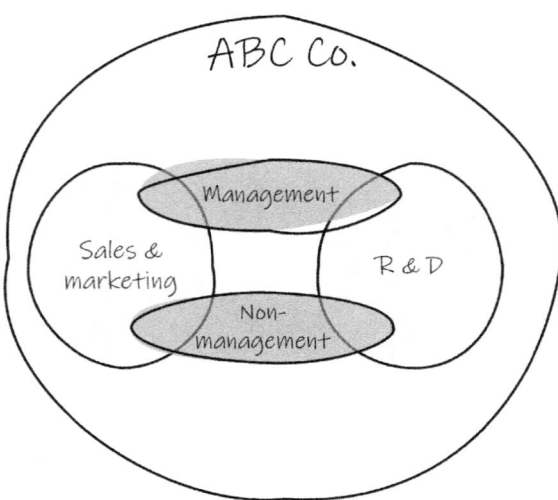

The system within ABC Company is also affected, maybe even regulated, by other systems. There may be a board of directors that sets the strategic direction of the organization. The company operates within a geographic area or areas and that community may have a certain culture or expectations about how the organization operates within it. There are customers and their needs and expectations of your products and services are likely evolving with time. The company is part of a particular industry and within that industry there will be competitors as well as laws and regulations with which the company must comply.

126

## WHY IS LOOKING AT MY COMPANY (OR TEAM) AS A SYSTEM IMPORTANT?

When you understand the system and how each of the elements within the system work (or don't work) together, you can be more effective in your role as a leader. For example, if you're developing a new product at ABC Company, you will need to know what's happening in other parts of the system. What are competitors working on? What are our customers looking for? What kinds of regulations must we comply with? What is ABC Company's capacity to develop, manufacture and market the product? Does this align with our strategic plan? What communication must exist between corporate silos to maximize our return on investing in this new product?

The better you understand the system, the better equipped you will be to operate most effectively within the system and generate the outcomes you're looking for.

## FIGURE OUT THE SYSTEM

The good news is, you have the ability to understand the systems within which you live and work. The bad news is these systems are constantly changing in subtle ways, so the learning never stops.

The key to understanding a system is curiosity. Look at the system from different perspectives. Try to see the big picture as well as the individual parts. Look at cause and effect, as well as correlation between activities and behaviours. Look for patterns or trends. Notice how information flows through the system, what is shared and who controls it.

Most importantly, be open to questioning your own assumptions about the system. This might be the most difficult part of looking at a system. We naturally make assumptions about what we observe based on our own experience. These are mental models. Once we let go of the assumption that we understand what's happening, we can be curious about what's really happening. Let's look at an example.

Each quarter, Kelly is responsible for creating a slide deck for the CEO to deliver to employees in the company update. She reaches out to people throughout the company (the system) to gather information about progress towards corporate goals, events and activities. Most people provide information within the requested time frame to allow Kelly enough time to pull together the slides for the CEO to review and prepare for the update. However, one of the people Kelly must collect information from, Dan, is consistently late, which results in Kelly having to work at the last minute and late into the evening before each update presentation.

Kelly is frustrated and annoyed with Dan and assumes he has no respect for her or the work she has to do after he has provided the necessary information. This results in tension between the two of them and, furthermore, contributes to tension between their two departments.

Now, imagine Kelly lets go of this assumption and instead approaches the situation with curiosity.

Well before the deadline, Kelly sits down to talk to Dan about content she needs from him for the presentation. She asks him why it has been difficult to provide this to her in a timely manner. Dan explains to her that he wants to make sure the CEO has the most current information and waits until the last minute to ensure this happens.

At this point, Kelly works to influence the system.

Kelly explains to Dan how this affects her job. The two of them brainstorm a better way to ensure the CEO has the most current information, while also allowing Kelly enough time to put it into a format that's easy for employees to understand.

When Kelly lets go of her assumptions about Dan's behaviours and is curious, she is able to better understand what was happening in the system and work to improve it.

This example is a relatively small challenge within a large system and is easily remedied. It's not so simple to fix corporate-wide problems, but you can influence them and make improvements. As you do, you learn about how your adjustments affect the system, which will influence what you do in the future.

Your ability to navigate the system is increased the better you understand the system. If you can effectively navigate the system, you will be a better manager. If you can positively influence the system, you will be a better leader.

## ▓ REFLECTION QUESTIONS ▓

1.  Think about your organization as a system:
    *   What are the main processes and activities taking place within the system?
    *   Who is part of the system and what is their role within the system?
    *   What is the organizational structure of the system?
    *   What are the obvious cultural traits of the organization (positive or negative)?
    *   Is there special knowledge or information within the organization?
    *   How is this knowledge shared?
    *   What tools and technology are used within the system?
    *   What are the outcomes (including products and services) of the system?
    *   Who are the clients or customers of the system? What do they want? What do they expect?
    *   Is the organization regulated? If so, in what way?
    *   What are the strategies within the system? Do they work together or conflict?

2.  What gaps exist in your knowledge of the system and what questions do you need to ask to close those gaps?

3.  In what areas can you influence the system?

4.  How will you choose to influence the system?

# MIND THE GAP

# 19

## Planning and Achieving Corporate Goals

*"Our goals can only be reached through a vehicle of a plan, in which we must fervently believe, and upon which we must vigorously act. There is no other route to success."*

*Pablo Picasso*

The most effective way to harness all the knowledge and experience of your team to achieve goals is to engage them in the process from beginning to end.

## ARTICULATE THE VISION

Your employees won't know where they're supposed to go or where they need to focus their efforts unless you tell them. That vision may be designed by you as the leader of the team or come down from on high from a senior executive or CEO. Regardless, it's your job to make sure your employees understand the long-term vision.

Beyond the one-sentence vision statement the company has published on the website, it's about creating a picture of what the future looks like, for your team, and for your customers. Not once, but again and again; sometimes people get so caught up in the day-to-day activities that float the boat, they lose sight of where they're sailing.

## ENGAGING EMPLOYEES IN SETTING THE GOALS

If you haven't engaged your employees in setting the vision, you have an opportunity to engage them in deciding the best way to achieve the vision. Once employees know where you're going as an organization, ask them how they believe you can get there.

You and your leadership team may already have ideas about what the goals should be. Why wouldn't you? You're in charge, right? At this early point, it's less about what the goals are and more about the opportunity for employees to become invested in them. Look at it this way, when do you feel more motivated—when someone tells you what to do or when you decide to do something because you believe it's necessary to get where you want to go?

Engaging employees in setting the goals doesn't have to be a complicated or formal process. It might be a one-hour brainstorming meeting. You could also start with some draft goals and ask employees for feedback. This gives employees an opportunity to be heard and contribute to their overall engagement. It is important to note that engaging staff has to be sincere and not just lip service; listen to and consider their input. If you choose to disregard their input for legitimate reasons, explain why. The worst thing you can do is ask for input and then ignore it. This will only result in alienating your employees and destroying trust.

## BEST KIND OF GOALS

Good goal design can be best described as S.M.A.R.T. (Specific, Measurable, Attainable, Realistic and Time-bound) goals. There are many resources out there to help you set goals, but ones that have these essential elements will be the most achievable.

## SHARE THE GOALS

When you write down your own goals, you immediately increase the chances of achieving them. You increase your odds even more if you share your goals with other people. The same goes for leading others in achieving goals. Like the vision, make sure your team understands the goals. Give them the opportunity to ask questions. Work together to figure out the best way to achieve those goals. You may even want to post the goals, as well as the progress toward those goals, in a common space so employees can see them regularly and be inspired by the progress.

## LEVERAGE YOUR TEAM

Steve Jobs said, "It doesn't make sense to hire smart people and tell them what to do; we hire smart people so they can tell us what to do." You have a great opportunity as a leader to engage your employees in their work when you empower them to make decisions about how to achieve the goals.

Have conversations with your team. Ask them about what's possible. Find out what obstacles might get in the way and how you might work together to prevent or overcome those obstacles. Identify any risks and strategize how to mitigate those risks. Understand the strengths of the people on your team as well as their learning objectives, and then with their input, assign activities that align to these skill sets and learning goals.

## REVISIT AND UPDATE

Be cautious of falling into the two goal-setting errors of *launch 'n leave* and *abandonment*. *Launch'n'leave* is when you expend a significant amount of effort to roll out a particular program, such as customer service training, and then do nothing to nurture the program. In other words, after you launch the shiny new program, you discard it and let it die.

In *abandonment*, executive teams spend a significant amount of time and energy on a business plan only to put it on a shelf and then dust it off at the end of the year to see if they did what they said they were going to do. A plan is useless if you never look at it. Pick a timeline—monthly, quarterly, whatever makes sense—and revisit the plan. How are you tracking toward the plan? Do you need to allocate more time or resources to pursuing the plan? Do you need to change the plan?

Many organizations (and individuals) had plans for 2020, then the world was hit with a pandemic. Organizations either pivoted, quickly changing their plans, or they didn't, waiting for the world to get back to normal. A choice that has only led to unfulfilled goals and failure for many. While the COVID-19 pandemic is an extreme case, there are often unexpected events or issues that arise and must be addressed in some way. Make sure you're looking at your plan on a regular basis to verify you're on track and it still makes sense. Engage your employees in this activity as well.

## RECOGNIZE AND CELEBRATE

Almost as important as building and working the plan is celebrating your success and recognizing all the hard work it took to achieve it. Give credit where credit is due. Remember, the best leaders take the blame for failures and attribute the recognition for success to their employees.

It's important to reflect on the hard work it took to achieve the goals and celebration is another opportunity for employee engagement. There are many ways to celebrate, big and small—a gift card, a team lunch, a big party, a nice bonus. Keep in mind the personalities and preferences of the team you're celebrating with and plan activities or rewards that will suit them.

## IN SUMMARY

The bottom line for supporting your team to achieve goals is ongoing, two-way communication. Ask questions, listen to what they tell you, share information as often and clearly as you can. Keep the conversation going.

When things go wrong, it's quite often because there was a miscommunication or lack of communication. It just stands to reason that clear, consistent, ongoing communication will contribute to things going right.

## ■ REFLECTION QUESTIONS ■

1. Do I involve my staff in goal setting? If so, what have been the benefits? If not, how have I perhaps limited our team success?

2. How can I be more effective in communicating with my team about our goals?

3. What opportunities do I have to engage my team in setting and achieving goals?

4. What can I do to ensure my team clearly understands our goals?

5. How can reviewing our goals on a regular basis make us more effective?

# MIND THE GAP

## Getting Shit Done

*"The key is not to prioritize what's on your schedule, but to schedule your priorities."*

*Stephen Covey, author of*
*The 7 Habits of Highly Effective People*

Have you worked for a leader that left things to the last minute? Or one who struggled to organize their team and so tasks fell behind and key deadlines were not met? Strong time management and prioritization are critical skills for a successful leader to have. Not only is it important for the leader, but also for their team members.

You might assume leaders would be good at completing tasks and getting things done, whether it is on their own or with their team. The reality is that we all have our areas of strengths and challenges, and not all leaders are good at getting shit done.

So, what can a leader do to ensure that poor time management doesn't affect productivity and team effectiveness?

## CREATE A SYSTEM

Employees need to understand the organization, how things get done and what their role is. Effective leaders create time management tools, learn to prioritize, and delegate tasks to the right individuals within the team. It takes practice, trust, discipline and vulnerability to lead a productive team. There are organizational systems that you, as a leader, can build or have built for the team, and there are your own personal systems.

## PRIORITIZING

Whether you use a dry erase board—writing, erasing and revising throughout the day—or an electronic to-do list, or a paper day planner, find the system that works for you.

## DOUG'S EXPERIENCE

*Time management is key to successfully getting things done. A strategy that I have adopted over the past couple of years is to plan out my week at the start of the work week (some people do this Friday at the end of the day) and list the tasks needed to be done as well as any projects we are working on. Tasks range from meetings I need to attend to checking in with staff regarding the projects we are working on. I learned the A-B-C system to help me prioritize.*

*Once you have created your list of tasks for the week, you prioritize and rank which tasks are high priority and need to be done ASAP (A), which tasks are high priority but are not urgent (B), and which tasks need to be done but, at the moment, there is not a sense of urgency on the timeline (C). I take the information and I enter it into my online calendar as well as my paper day planner to help me time block out my week. Every morning, I review my day planner and review the specific to-do tasks for the day. I try to stay true to my planner, but I also recognize that the plan is fluid and that some things that are not high priority and urgent may be moved to the next day.*

Having the mindset that your planner is fluid allows you to deal with unexpected situations that can occur without causing you stress. Take the time to see if there is anything on your list that can be delegated to your team. A good example of a task you may rank urgent (A) could be approving a budget. Your team may be waiting for approval for the budget in order to move forward. Rate this task as an A; otherwise, you are holding up the team.

# TIME BLOCKING FOR TIME MANAGEMENT

If you have created a system and prioritized, but still struggle to find out why you do not have time to do all the things you need to complete, consider a time motion study to help you effectively manage your time. A time motion study allows you to track what you are doing for the week. List your activities and the time you've spent on them. Once you see where your time is being spent, it allows you to adjust accordingly. You may be surprised at how effectively or ineffectively you are using your time. Maybe you are spending more time on your C tasks which have to be done but are not urgent or you are spending time on something you could easily delegate to your team. We often can feel that there is not enough time in the day to get things done but a time motion study can help you pinpoint potential areas that you may be under or over-utilizing.

## HEATHER'S EXPERIENCE

*Until I started time blocking, I was feeling overworked and exhausted. As a leader with hyper-achieving tendencies, I take on several projects and join many committees. I believe I am a great multi-tasker and I cannot help volunteering for things. It is a running joke in my house. I attended a meeting for Women in Leadership and was curious about how to start a chapter in Edmonton. Next thing you know I am now the Chair of Women in Leadership - Alberta Chapter.*

*Before I mastered time blocking, I was running two different Google calendars as well as two different day planners, one set for my coaching practice and the other for my 9-5 career. Now, I use a two-step process. I sit down on Sunday and plan out my week and review my calendar. I look at the tasks and prioritize using an A-B-C system. "A" items are things that are on the top of my priority list. These are my non-negotiables for the week and have to get done first. My "B" items are important and should be done by Friday. My "C" items are nice to do but not urgent.*

*Next, I time block my items, leaving room for unexpected high priority tasks. Then if something unexpected comes up, I have room in my calendar to address it.*

Using a system provides you a clear picture of the daily, weekly, and monthly tasks and an unhurried opportunity to delegate more effectively to your team members. Remember, people want to feel like a valuable part of the team and positively contribute to the overall success, but they don't want your ineffective time management to result in tasks dropping in their laps at the last minute.

## SETTING REALISTIC DEADLINES

Setting realistic deadlines is critical to reaching your goals. In your leadership role, you have many things on your plate you are trying to juggle. If you don't set realistic deadlines, it becomes easy for you to push timelines back, which can make you late or even miss a goal. Setting deadlines is a great way to hold yourself accountable and allows you to focus on the desired task at hand. Being more intentional with how you spend your time allows you to meet deadlines on time.

For example, a leader has a number of projects that his team is working on but he has not checked in to make sure that everything is running smoothly. Two days before the projects are due, he checks in with his team and finds that there are some key elements missing and the deadline for the project is looming. The team needs to work overtime in order to meet the deadline and the leader knows that this is not their best work. If he had set up accountability check-ins throughout the project, these key issues would have been addressed. If they had planned the work well in advance of the deadline, setting aside chunks of time to complete tasks, the end result would be of higher quality. Procrastination is not our friend, often results in our inability to get things done and negatively impacts the quality of work.

Flexibility is also important when we set deadlines. Sometimes when we begin a task, we realize that it may require more time than we originally planned so we need to be able to re-adjust priorities and the timeline to meet our goal. As a leader, we need to learn to be flexible with ourselves and our teams, and adapt when needed— both qualities of a leader with high emotional intelligence.

## DELEGATING

Delegating tasks within your team is crucial to getting things done. Remember, you are a team, and you do not have to do everything on your own. The team will be expecting you to delegate the tasks. Each team member comes with their own unique gifts and talents, and most members are looking for opportunities to continue to grow professionally. Make sure you know what your teams' gifts and talents are so you can provide them with opportunities to continue to grow and develop their skills. Reflect back on your career when you were eager to take on leadership responsibilities, whether they were formal or informal roles. You were in their shoes at some point and eager to stretch yourself. When you delegate tasks, you empower your staff by making them feel valued. Valued employees want to work hard for you and the organization. Do not stay tucked away in your office, working away on tasks that could and should be delegated.

## IT IS THE LEADER'S RESPONSIBILITY TO GET IT DONE

At the end of the day, the leader is accountable to ensure that there is progress toward the organizational goals. An ineffective leader can wreak havoc within an organization by their inability to get things done—missed deadlines, undervalued staff, high staff absences, high staff turnover and financial losses.

The effect on the team of a lack of effective time management systems and practices is guaranteed to lower levels of employee engagement. The perception of the team by others outside of the group might be one of dysfunction. A leader must take time management and getting shit done seriously.

## NOW WHAT?

A good place to start when you are struggling to get shit done is to start with time management and adopt a system that is going to work for you. Still struggling? Taking the time to do a time motion study is a great option and something you can easily do yourself.

Learn to prioritize, plan and delegate the tasks that need to be completed. Having trouble letting go of some tasks? Start with baby steps and set up accountability check-ins to ensure things are on track. Empowering your staff and creating trust goes a long way. If you can't let go of things, you will find yourself becoming overwhelmed with all of the tasks you need to get done.

If you haven't taken the time to connect with your staff, now is the time to do that. Make sure you know what their gifts and talents are and how you can use their skills to help meet deadlines. When you move into a new team, interview each staff member to learn more about them. Ask them about their strengths, areas where they would like to grow, career aspirations and what they would like more of in their job. It is a great way to gain greater insight into the team dynamics.

Identify any gaps in the skill set of the team and look for professional development solutions that will support your team's ability to perform efficiently as possible. When hiring your next team member, consider the skills they bring and what tasks they are a match for when you delegate.

## ■ REFLECTION QUESTIONS ■

1.  On a scale of 1-10, where would you rate your ability to get shit done?

2.  What are the time management tools you use? How could they be more effective?

3.  What is an area that you could work on that would help you get shit done?

4.  Moving forward, what action could you implement tomorrow to increase productivity?

5.  What strategies do you use to learn about the strengths of your team members?

# Leading Change

> *"A genuine leader is not a searcher for consensus
> but a molder of consensus."*
>
> *Martin Luther King Jr.*

Sometimes leaders know change is necessary. They often sit through important meetings and make big decisions. Then they come out of those meetings, go back to their desks and ask or tell employees to do things differently. What is often not considered is that they've had these discussions and probably put a great deal of thought into the change. They've already invested a significant amount of time and effort into the change, whatever it is. Then, in what may seem to their team as coming out of the blue, the leader announces to employees that they must stop what they're doing today and do something different tomorrow.

Some people can handle this. However, many may be rocked by the announcement.

## YOUR ROLE AS A LEADER

Larger organizations may have in-house experts to provide project management or change management support. If this is the case in your organization, take advantage of their expertise and experience. However, even with these experts to guide the process, you still have a large role as a leader in creating and supporting change. Your role is one of the most significant in terms of the impact on the organization's performance, as you have the most direct influence on the employees you manage. Recognize the importance of engaging your employees through the change process. If you take just one thing away from this chapter, let it be this: the success of organizational change depends on the behaviour of your frontline employees.

There are a couple of things to consider here. First, your conversations with your employees, either one-on-one or in a team, are an opportunity to really listen to your employees and understand their goals, strengths, frustrations and opportunities. Overall, when an employee feels seen, heard and understood, they are more engaged. This is true in day-to-day life as well as through times of change.

The second thing to consider is your own self-awareness. How do you feel about the change and how are your words and actions demonstrating your feelings to your employees? If you say, "Yeah, I know this is stupid, but we have to do it because the big guy said so," how motivated do you think employees are going to be in embracing the change?

A manager's desire to change directly influences an employee's desire to support the change. If you're not on board, your team won't be either. If you aren't on board, consider what you might need to shift your mindset. Do you need more information? Do you need your manager to see, hear, and understand you? Do you need coaching from a manager or peer?

Leadership doesn't happen by accident. It takes work. You can choose to be a positive influence, acting as a change champion and supporting others through the change, or a negative influence, resisting change.

## LEVERAGE AVAILABLE TOOLS AND MODELS

There are a number of change management models. For example, in psychologist Kurt Lewin's model, change involves three stages: Unfreezing, Change, and Refreeze. Another change management methodology, The Transition Model, developed by change consultant

William Bridge, also proposes three stages: Ending, Losing, and Letting Go; The Neutral Zone; and The New Beginning.

No matter what you call it or how many steps you want to include, the simplest way to think about change is these three phases: Current State, Transition or Change State, and Future State.

|  | Current State | Transition or Change State | Future State |
|---|---|---|---|
| Lewin | Unfreezing | Change | Refreeze |
| Bridge | Ending, Losing, and Letting Go | The Neutral Zone | The New Beginning |

Identifying the **current state** is the most straightforward phase. It's what things look like now, but it's also about knowing that things need to change. Employee engagement during this time might include meeting with employees to describe the change we're trying to make, while also helping employees to understand the need for the change. This is a good time for leaders to be curious about what employees are thinking and feeling.

The **transition phase** is a necessary evil. It's uncomfortable and often bumpy. This is the most difficult stage of change and where you can expect to focus your change efforts. The good news is, there are plenty of tools you can leverage to help you get through this stage. (For example, the Prosci model of change management which includes the five steps of a change process: Awareness, Desire, Knowledge, Action and Reinforcement (or ADKAR). Prosci offers a number of tools and templates to help organizations navigate change.)

Finally, you arrive at the **future state**.

It's important to ensure your employees understand what the change will be, how it might affect their jobs, what will be expected of them during the transition state, and what that future state will look like.

## ENGAGE EARLY

Imagine, for a moment, that your life partner comes home from work one day and announces, without any prior discussion, "I've bought a new house. We're moving tomorrow."

For a few of you, this may be an exciting announcement and you start immediately searching online for moving boxes. However, for most of us, an announcement like this would be shocking, upsetting and maybe the beginning of a legal separation. You would probably expect this kind of change would only happen after hours of discussion, multiple viewings, maybe a meeting with the bank and some agreement on what you're looking for in a home.

Now imagine how your employees might feel when you announce a change that will affect how they do their work every day. That's why the earlier you start to engage employees in the change, the more effectively you can incorporate the change.

## ARTICULATE AND SHARE THE VISION

As a leader, you must be able to share the vision, whether it's yours or someone from senior leadership such as the CEO or a Board of Directors. If you can't make it clear to your team where they're going, they'll have a hard time getting there.

The key is to share the vision often, in different ways and consistently until it is achieved. For example, sharing it at the beginning of a change and then never again won't be effective. You'll need to share it as often as you have the opportunity, in one-on-one meetings, team meetings and other corporate gatherings.

It's also important to share the vision in different ways. People have various preferences when it comes to receiving and understanding information. Some prefer brief messages in an email, while others might want to have the opportunity to discuss the information and ask questions. If you communicate in a variety of different ways, you are more likely to be effective in sharing that vision with all employees.

Finally, consistency is king—or queen. Obviously if your message keeps changing, employees will become confused. Furthermore, if the message differs between leaders across the organization, you may come against challenges, especially if it's integral for different departments to work together to achieve the vision.

## BE THE CHANGE CHAMPION THAT PEOPLE WILL TRUST

Because change is hard and the desire to change is very personal, it is vital for leaders to establish trust. Especially when you're at the beginning of change and as you're helping people to accept the change, people must trust you and they must also trust the vision of the future state.

Here are some ways to nurture trust through change:

- Share information. Be transparent, even if you don't have all the answers—if there is a gap of information, people will fill it with speculation and rumours.
- Take time to nurture relationships: if your employees are worried about change, take more time with them.
- Listen. Don't just hear them but be curious, ask questions. If you engage people and then don't take their suggestions, let them know why.
- Give people discretion in how they do their jobs whenever it's possible—give them some control.
- Recognize their efforts, particularly when it supports the change efforts.

## HELP OTHERS UNDERSTAND THE NEED FOR CHANGE

People are only motivated to change if they understand why change is necessary. When leaders begin to talk about change with employees, they start to create a shared awareness of the current state and the need for change. In conversations with employees, leaders have an opportunity to not only describe the change they're trying to make, but to help employees independently realize the need for change.

For example, in the current state, we can ask questions like:

- What's going well right now?
- What could be going better?

- Tell me what you know about our competitors? What are they doing to serve their customers?
- What do our members or customers need from us? What do they want from us?

## LEADING CHANGE INTO THE TRANSITION PHASE

When you start to move from the current state into the transition state, things get more complicated. The work to implement change becomes more difficult and requires strategy. Remember, this is the necessary evil we must go through to move from the current state to the future state.

It's like exercise. Imagine someone's current physical state is out of shape. Maybe they get winded climbing a flight of stairs, or have gotten a bit rounder due to eating too many delicious treats. People can't just cross their fingers and hope to arrive at some kind of fit and toned future state. (Wouldn't that be great?)

There needs to be a transition state including exercise and more healthy choices. Some days we're very disciplined and others, not so much. But if we don't make the effort and put in the work, we will never arrive at the desired future state. And frankly, some of us have no desire to do the work to make that change. So how do we get people to want to do the work to make the change? How do we influence the desire to change?

One way to do this is through conversations. As a leader, you have an opportunity to help people move from knowing that things have to change to wanting to change.

Desire is personal. Ultimately, you can't make anyone decide to buy in. You can only understand their barriers and attempt to remove them. You can tell people that the change is good but you're more likely to get buy-in when they see it for themselves. Your conversations with employees might include questions like:

- What is at stake if nothing changes?
- What is the urgency?
- What's standing in our way?
- What's the first step?

## SELL THE BENEFIT OF CHANGE

"Why" can be a powerful motivator. For example, maybe your organization is going through a large software change. It will take significant time and effort and employees will have to learn the new system and change their workflow. However, the new software will allow employees to better serve customers, which will also result in attracting new customers, which means more revenue for the company, which might even mean better pay or a big bonus. There are four motivating reasons to support the change. Look for the benefits to provide your employees with "whys" to support the change in your organization.

*What's In it For Me?* This probably isn't the first time you've heard WIIFM but it's worth mentioning. Because the desire to change is so personal, your employees will want to know how the change will impact them and their job.

You can tell them what the future state has to offer them. Maybe it's increased efficiency which will make their jobs easier in the long run, maybe there will be more opportunities for them to grow, develop and even advance. What is even more powerful than telling them, however, is to help them discover it for themselves by asking questions that make people focus on the future and what might be in it for them personally. For example:

- Where would you like to be in the future state?
- What opportunities might you see for yourself?
- What role would you like to play in the transition?
- What could you gain from that experience?

## IDENTIFY RESISTANCE AND MANAGE IT

With any change, you will likely find there are some people who will be quite resistant. This can be challenging because, as you recall, successful change happens when you have buy-in from frontline employees.

The only way to effectively manage resistance is to first understand it. Here are some reasons employees may resist change:

Pride: perhaps an employee is particularly proud of the current state. Maybe they were part of creating the old system.

Fear: maybe they're afraid of the unknown. In the future state, they may not be perceived as the expert as they may have been in the past. Maybe they fear their job will become less rewarding or even irrelevant in the future state.

Doubt: they may believe the change will not make a positive difference for them or achieve the claimed outcome. They may see it as a flavour of the month, claiming "We've heard it all before" or "It's just another program." This is especially true of long-term employees who bring a significant amount of knowledge, experience and value, but also have corporate memory of less than successful change attempts in the past.

It's helpful to understand where your employees might be in terms of change. In your conversations, identify:

- Are they still in the beginning stage where they don't really understand the need for change?
- Do they understand the change but maybe don't know where they fit in or what to do?
- Are they working on new skills so they can implement the change?
- Are they fully on board and acting as change champions?

When you understand where people are in terms of accepting change, you can help them move forward with coaching and communication.

## GATHER SUPPORT

There's no reason for you to lead change alone. Recruit change champions to help you implement changes in your organization. These are employees who will advocate for change and even support other employees to change. This is an opportunity for you to offer a new challenge to employees who are looking for more in their job. By engaging them in the change, you're also engaging them in their work, contributing to their growth and, likely, retaining them as employees.

Another hint here is to include those employees who may be most resistant to change. Rather than allowing them to be roadblocks, getting them involved early and asking for their input makes them advocates.

The bottom line is that change is hard. It's even harder when you're a leader trying to implement change within an organization with individuals who may not be inclined to change themselves. The good news is there are plenty of things you can do to make sure your employees understand the vision, why it's important and what they need to do to make the transition to the future state.

## ■ REFLECTION QUESTIONS ■

1. Think about an organizational change you've gone through.

   - What was your role?
   - What did you notice about how the leaders managed the change?
   - What went well and what could have been better?

2. Think about the organization you are currently in.

   - What are the changes I need to implement in my organization (big or small)?
   - How can the ideas shared in this chapter help me to implement these changes?

# MIND THE GAP

# Leading Through Adversity

*"Adversity causes some men to break,
and others to break records."*

William Arthur Wad, author of *Thoughts of a Christian Optimist*

## LEADING IN A CRISIS

Leading when things are going well is relatively easy. That fact becomes very apparent once a crisis occurs. However, a crisis is an opportunity for a leader to shine. Many leaders emerge when given an opportunity to showcase their skills during times of adversity, crisis, or chaos. As cliché as it may sound, leading in times of adversity can be a gift and should be viewed as an opportunity to explore new ideas, learn and grow.

Leading in a crisis requires some additional skills and behaviours that may not be as important when things are going well. These are behaviours like maintaining a calm, clear head under stress, connecting with people who themselves may be facing stress or even trauma, and communicating in a clear, concise and consistent manner about very difficult topics. *Keep Calm and Carry On*, a phrase first used on a motivational poster produced by the British government in 1939 in preparation for World War II, is probably one of the most important things a leader can do during challenging times. Calmness, a positive attitude, and confidence are infectious, but so too are panic and thoughtless reactions. Be a leader who sets the example for others to follow and who will support your team to have the best opportunity for success.

Following are some ways you can draw on your leadership in times of crisis.

## BE PREPARED

There is always potential for a crisis to occur. Perhaps it's financial, as we've seen throughout history, such as recessions and depressions. Maybe it's violence that impacts entire communities, like school shootings or acts of terrorism. It might be a natural disaster, such as an earthquake, tornado, or flooding. There is potential for technology to fail or secure information to be leaked or hacked. The worldwide coronavirus pandemic put the world on its knees. The list goes on and will continue to expand into the future. The point is, while you may not be able to predict a crisis, you can count on one occurring at some point and there are ways to be prepared.

One way to do this is to review history. Look at crises of the past and the leaders who rose through them. For example, if we take a look at the COVID pandemic, we see countries whose leaders took swift action to reduce the spread of the virus while others dismissed it and their citizens suffered the consequences.

While you may not know exactly what might come in terms of a crisis, you do know what types of crisis might occur, especially in relation to your business. Consider some worst-case scenarios and then make plans to respond to them. For example, what if your physical space is no longer available? What if one or many of your key people become incapacitated? What if you lose business from half of your clients in a short period of time? What if you're unable to produce your product?

Bring your team together to discuss these scenarios and how you might respond to them. Create a plan and prepare your team. Then keep that plan up to date so when you need it, you can implement it quickly and minimize the impact of the crisis on your team and organization.

Don't underestimate the potential damage a crisis can do to your team, your company, or even the world. The worst can happen and being prepared will help you demonstrate leadership when it does. If you have plans, teams, and key messages sitting on a shelf, ready to be put into action should a crisis occur, you'll be able to respond swiftly when it does.

## MAKE YOUR PEOPLE YOUR TOP PRIORITY

When you prepare for any crisis, consider that leaders must put people first. It's not just the right thing to do, it's integral for your company's reputation, as well as your reputation as a leader. Before you take any action in response to a crisis, ensure your team is safe and well. If they aren't, they should be your first area of concern. Take the time to connect with your team. Seek to understand what has happened and how it may have affected them. When your employees know they are your priority, they'll stick with you through the crisis and beyond.

## OPEN, HONEST COMMUNICATION

Trust is easy to break and very hard to rebuild. You will never hold the trust of your employees and customers if you're not open and honest with them. Here are some things to consider:

- If you don't provide information, people tend to fill the gaps with their own, often inaccurate, information. When you communicate early, you control the message.
- It's okay to admit you don't have all the answers. In fact, it's better to admit your shortcomings or lack of knowledge than let them be pointed out or revealed by others.
- When you take ownership, you are demonstrating leadership. When you point fingers and blame others, you are demonstrating cowardice.

Communication must be timely, appropriate for the audience, and regular and ongoing. There will, undoubtedly, be a need for more frequency of communication than what might be normal for your organization or work unit. It is critical for you not to fall into the trap of communicating only by email. Your team will want to see the whites of your eyes. Your calm presence in the face of adversity will give them reassurance.

## ADDRESS THE PROBLEM HEAD ON

If your goal is to demonstrate leadership in the face of adversity, then you certainly don't want to hide when the time comes. When you're overwhelmed by a significant event or crisis, natural human instincts kick in and it's fight or flight. Choose to fight.

Take a moment to absorb what has happened, then pull those plans off the shelf and put them into action. Check in with your people, rally the troops and respond, rather than react, to the situation with which you're faced.

## EXPECT SETBACKS

There may be setbacks when you are leading through times of adversity. That is to be expected. Your team will appreciate your ability to make decisions (even if those decisions are imperfect) and take action (as long as you stand behind those actions and own whatever consequences there may be.) Your team and those around you will forgive wrong decisions if they were made in good faith, with the best information available at the time.

It will be important for you and your team to address setbacks head on, deal with them quickly, learn from them and move onto the next issue.

## RECOGNIZE THE PEOPLE

Just as it is important to look after your people through a crisis, it will be important to recognize their hard work and commitment. During a crisis, you may need to ask your people to work longer hours or take on tasks outside of their area of expertise. You may ask them to put themselves into stressful or even dangerous situations. Make sure you show your appreciation for their willingness to do what was requested. People want to feel valued and appreciated, especially when they've gone above and beyond.

## TAKE CARE OF YOURSELF

If you're not well, you can't lead others. As a leader, you need to take care of yourself before you can take care of others. This is true anytime but especially during challenging times. A healthy mindset coming into a period of adversity or organizational stress will more likely contribute to a positive outcome. Our wellness contributes to our resiliency. Be aware of how your wellness, or lack of, is affecting your leadership.

### KERI'S EXPERIENCE

*I recall a time when I was in a leadership position. As an employee, I was feeling undervalued and unappreciated and I was generally unhappy in my role. I wasn't learning or growing, and I certainly didn't feel seen, heard or understood. I felt stuck and I no longer looked forward to coming to work. Some days, I even dreaded it. At the end of each day, I would go home feeling drained and exhausted. I had no energy left to offer my family, never mind face additional stress or adversity.*

*While it was difficult, I recognized I was not able to be the leader I wanted to be for the people who reported to me. Although I was still able to offer my team my time and attention, I was neither optimistic nor inspiring. That's when I knew I had to make a change. I needed to take care of myself so that I could be the best leader for others, even if that meant leaving my team.*

If you come up against a crisis when you don't have any reserves left, you certainly won't be able to lead anyone else through the crisis. As a leader, as a person, you must take care of you.

## ▥ REFLECTION QUESTIONS ▥

1.  What kind of leader do you want to be when faced with adversity?

2.  When have you observed or provided leadership during adversity?

    -   What went well?
    -   What could have gone better?

- What can you take away from that experience to prepare you for the next time?

3. What can you do today to prepare for an inevitable crisis?
4. What do you want people to say about you when the crisis is over?
5. What will you do to give them reason to say those things?

# Working for a Bad Boss

*"You got to know when to hold 'em, know when to fold 'em...know when to walk away, and know when to run."*

**From the Kenny Roger's song, The Gambler,
written by songwriter Don Schlitz**

As you move through your leadership journey, you will have the opportunity to work with many types of individuals. You will get along with some of them and others you may not. Hopefully in your career, you will work with more people you get along with than you don't. As leaders, we want to create a positive work culture where employees feel empowered and valued members of the team. But if our leadership style clashes with that of our boss, creating this positive work environment may be more difficult.

It is important to have a good relationship with your boss—even if you find them challenging to get along with—as this relationship can impact your current role within the organization and may even impact potential opportunities for advancement and the trajectory of your career within the organization if your boss refuses to empower you or give you effective feedback.

Unfortunately, your fate may be controlled by your boss at this point in your career and they can make your job rewarding or they can make your job quite difficult.

## WHAT ARE SOME CHARACTERISTICS OF A BAD BOSS?

Sometimes we end up working with a bad or difficult boss. Maybe you have a boss that micromanages your team, or takes credit for the team's work, maybe they play favorites, or are always absent when you need them. They could also be poor listeners, manage by fear, have no follow-through or use a top-down management style. Whatever describes your boss, you need to learn how to work with these scenarios.

A theory within Positive Intelligence (PQ) is to look at challenging experiences as gifts and opportunities for learning and growth. You, as the leader, need to look for the gift or opportunity of working with a challenging boss. How can you use this experience to help you grow as a leader? Instead of letting yourself get stuck in the muck and fall into a negative thinking loop, you can reframe situations that you find extremely frustrating and shift to a more positive mindset. Each experience is a gift and opportunity to better ourselves and when we change our thought patterns and begin to reframe, we become more empathetic to that person. When we treat people with empathy, we see their actions in a different light and can begin building stronger relationships with them.

### HEATHER'S EXPERIENCE

*I worked with a colleague who was really struggling with her boss and often found herself ruminating about her situation. When her thoughts fixated on his negative behaviours, she quickly found herself feeling like she was working in a toxic environment. She felt that people were disconnected, everyone was doing their own thing, and it was a negative working environment. My friend was not sure how to resolve these thoughts. One day her boss did something that upset her, and in her mind, that was the final straw. She told him exactly how she felt about him, and the end result was not good. Her boss was shocked as he had no idea this was how she felt. She left the organization shortly after that. I can't help but wonder how the outcome would have been different if she had talked to him earlier and addressed her concerns.*

*What is the lesson here? We all have choices that we can make and at times, we can find ourselves taking on the victim or 'poor me' role. I worked with a coach (yes, coaches have coaches) and she reminded me that WE choose how we want to show up. Big a-ha moment! We can waste a lot of time and energy getting stuck in the muck of negativity or we can learn to release those feelings and see how your perspective shifts to a more positive mindset.*

*I was going through a challenging situation at work at the same time my friend was thinking about leaving her job. It was the first time in my career that I really dreaded going into work; but reframing my thoughts allowed me to create a growth mindset. Repeating to myself, "I choose how I am going to show up in this situation" allowed me to reframe the situation in my mind. These words that I repeated over and over were magical to me and shifted me to a more positive mindset. Since that time, I have used that mantra many times when I have been going into a confrontational setting. It has helped me enter challenging situations in a more positive frame of mind. It has allowed me to go into difficult meetings with a professional demeanor and show up as my best self at work. It has allowed me to ground myself and empowered me to keep that thought top of mind moving forward. The next time you are going into a difficult situation, I challenge you to take a deep breath and repeat that sentence, "I choose how I am going to show up today."*

Life is full of ups and downs and one thing that is important for us to recognize is that there are things in life we can control, things we have a bit of control over, and things we have no control over. As a leader, it is important to recognize these factors. If you are in a situation with a difficult boss, take a moment and list the things that you can control. Remember, all the other things are out of your control. When you write it down, it allows you to have a better perspective of the situation. You control how you show up and how you react to situations.

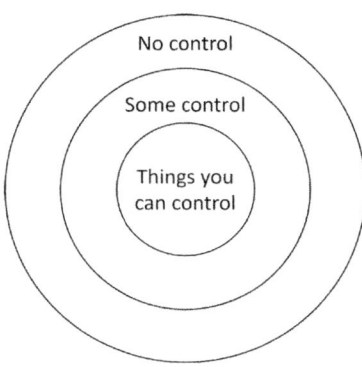

## STRATEGIES TO SUCCEED IN THE CURRENT ROLE

Here are some ideas that you may find helpful in dealing with a difficult boss:

1. Find opportunities to build a relationship with your boss
2. Ask for what you need
3. Offer feedback when opportunities present
4. Talk to someone in your union or in your Human Resources department

## BUILD A RELATIONSHIP WITH YOUR BOSS

Take the time to get to know your boss. Creating a connection or finding something that you can talk to your boss about can help to develop and nurture your relationship. Try to support their successes and learn to work around their perceived weaknesses. If your boss struggles with planning, offer to take the lead on the next project. Instead of complaining about one of his areas of weakness, work to help him. Remember, your boss is a person just like you and me. They have hopes and dreams just like you do. Try to figure out what they value in their role and how you can support them in fulfilling that value. Spending time with them on a personal level may give you a different perspective about them and their role as a leader.

## ASK FOR WHAT YOU NEED

If your boss doesn't know what you need, they are unable to provide it. If you need more communication or information, ask for it. If you need more training or support, make a case for it. If your boss isn't available or accessible when you need, ask when the best time might be to connect. If you have certain expectations of your boss, you must share them or you may experience disappointment. Your boss is not a mind reader and may not even be aware that there is a problem or an unmet expectation.

## OFFER FEEDBACK

To be fair, offering feedback to your boss may not be an option. There are people who don't want to hear it and are not prepared to be that vulnerable. However, there are other leaders who want to improve and just aren't aware of their blind spots. They may not know how their behavior is impacting you or the rest of your team.

Be courageous—and diplomatic—when you point out to your boss the behavior that's impacting you negatively. In this case, it may be helpful to practice this conversation with someone safe before taking it to the boss. Your Human Resources department might be able to support you with this conversation or a coach can work with you to prepare.

## SPEAK TO OTHERS

If you are in a situation where you are being bullied or harassed by your boss, consider letting someone else know. In Canada, there are laws to protect people from bullying and harassment in the workplace. You have the right to a workplace free of harassment. If you believe that you're being harassed or bullied according to the law, make sure you are documenting any occurrences of harassment or bullying behavior. Note the date and description of the behavior, and also if anyone else was present to observe or hear the incident. Then get someone else involved. Whether it's a union representative or a person in your human resources department, make sure you're letting others know about the situation.

If these three strategies do not work, you need to begin to recognize when it is time to go. You may have opportunities to move within your organization or you can work on how to leave on good terms.

## TAKE CARE OF YOURSELF

Working in an unhealthy environment may have negative impacts on your mental well being. Determine what the cost is to you personally if things do not change (not just the financial cost in lost opportunities but the cost to your mental and physical health).

Stress can be extremely hard on your body and can show up in multiple ways. You may feel exhausted, demotivated, and have trouble sleeping. It can show up in somatic ways as well such as stomach pains, headaches, or an achy body. Stress can even lead to potential burnout. Picture going to work every day for a year and living in a toxic environment. What is the impact not only on your professional life but also on your personal life? What is the cost to your overall wellness in this case? Is it worth the cost?

If you are still unable to resolve the challenges with your boss, an option may be to begin to look for opportunities within your organization or even another company. You may have been contemplating gaining more experience in a different area within the organization and this may be the opportune time to begin looking. As a leader, it could be a perfect time to do an inventory of your skills and reflect upon your areas of growth. This could help you if you decide to look at other positions. Start with talking to your talent management team or HR department. If there is nothing within your organization, perhaps reach out to a head-hunter to see what potential career opportunities might be out there. Talk to other individuals who work in your industry and leverage your network to uncover opportunities and to find out who may be hiring at the moment.

## CREATE A TRANSITION PLAN

If you really are unhappy, it may be time to begin to create an exit strategy. Trying to figure out what is next can be confusing, stressful, and time-consuming, and partnering with an Executive Coach can help you gain clarity and purpose as you move forward. Working with a coach can help you begin to plan for the next steps on your terms and move the process of transition along faster.

Determine what type of work you're looking for and what kind of organization you'd like to work for. Make sure you know what the core values and beliefs are of the organization and if they align with your own core values and beliefs. Build your resume with that in mind. It can be scary to make the transition but nothing on our leadership path is certain. Stretching ourselves to move to a new position helps us grow and develop into the leader we want to be.

## HEATHER'S EXPERIENCE

*As a coach, I worked with a client who was really unhappy in her current role. She had worked for an organization for over 20 years and, over the last few years, felt a growing sense of discontent. Once we began to explore her core values and beliefs, she recognized that her current values and beliefs did not align with the values and beliefs of the organization she worked for. It was like a light bulb went off for her. What she felt was once an open system, where collaboration and sharing of ideas was valued and encouraged, had now become an organization that was micro-managed with a focus on a top-down management style. With that in mind, she updated her resume and began to apply for other positions. She quickly found an organization that aligned with her core values and beliefs. Her one regret was that she had not made the move sooner. Through coaching, she was able to recognize that even though leaving her 20-year job was terrifying, living a life where she could feel happy and fulfilled was more important.*

## LEAVE ON GOOD TERMS

It's important to leave with dignity and on good terms with your boss, colleagues, and organization. Your reputation will follow you and it's better to be viewed in a positive light. Create your leaving story. For example, rather than telling others you're leaving because your boss is a tyrant and you can't take it anymore, tell people you're ready for the next step in your career. Although it's very tempting to spill the truth about how you feel, when you speak negatively about others, it reflects poorly on you.

## NOW WHAT?

Working with a bad boss may have a negative impact on one's overall professional and personal wellbeing. When we are caught in a negative place, it is important to do an inventory or check-in to reflect what our role was in this situation or what we could have done differently. Is there an opportunity to learn from this situation so that we can add this to our toolbox? What has this situation stretched us to do that promotes positive growth? Determine what is important to you and how you can resolve the situation to best meet your needs.

## ■ REFLECTION QUESTIONS ■

If you are in a relationship with a bad boss:

1. How have you tried to improve your relationship with your boss?

2. What is the personal cost to your wellbeing if you continue to work in a toxic environment?

3. How is this scenario impacting your personal and professional relationships?

4. What is holding you back from making a change?

# The Leader's Role In Corporate Culture

*"Culture eats strategy for breakfast."*

**Peter Drucker, best-selling author and
management thought leader**

The simplest way to describe culture is *the way we do things around here*. Culture exists whether your company creates it intentionally or not. Culture contributes, positively or negatively, to a company's financial results. A culture can be constructive, where employees work together effectively to achieve the organization's goals. Conversely, a culture can be toxic, where employees cannot work together effectively, are likely unhappy and disgruntled and the organization is challenged to effectively achieve its goals.

In 2021, Gallup released its *State of the Global Workplace* report which suggested that worldwide, only 20% of employees are engaged at work—highly involved in and enthusiastic about their work and workplace. In the United States and Canada, that number is higher, 34%, but that still leaves 66% of employees who are not engaged and not working to their full potential.

In their 2017 *State of the Global Workplace* study, Gallup reported companies in the top 25% of employee engagement also reported 17% higher productivity, 10% higher customer metrics, 20% more sales, and 21% greater profitability. These companies also experienced 41% lower absenteeism, 40% fewer quality incidents and 70% fewer employee safety incidents.

Harris Interactive completed a study in 2012 and found most people (88%), and almost all executives (94%) believe culture is important to business success. In an 11-year study, Harvard Business School found that organizations focused on shaping their culture increased their net income by 756% over 11 years. Imagine a company has a net income of $100M annually. With a constructive corporate culture, they're able to grow that net income 756% over 11 years. That means in the 11th year, net income would be $800M. Investing in a strong culture pays off.

Let's look at the Gallup data. A company is getting the full return on their investment in employee salaries from only 34% of their people and getting only a partial return on that other 66%. If a company has 100 employees, and the average salary of those employees is $50K, the company is investing $5M in salaries annually. Of that $5M, $3M (66%) is allocated to a group of people who aren't fully engaged in their work. If you're going to invest that kind of money, wouldn't you want to get the most out of that investment?

What all this research tells us is that, if an organization can create a constructive corporate culture where employees are engaged, they can expect higher productivity and profitability.

Most companies have a strategic plan but not all have a culture strategy. Even those who do, struggle to achieve the ideal culture. That's because culture involves people and people are complicated. As a leader, you can have a significant influence on people, and therefore, the culture of your organization.

## KERI'S EXPERIENCE

*I worked for a company that prided itself on having a very constructive culture. They had proof. A survey to measure culture was conducted bi-annually. There were very high participation rates among employees and the results were very positive. (So much so, the company became a case study for the organization that was hired to conduct the assessment.) We had completed this survey for years. To be fair, we had made great strides in improving the culture over this time. A significant amount of focus and effort had been made to implement policies and programs that supported a more constructive culture.*

*While it was positive that we measured culture and put policies and practices in place to enhance the culture, there was still a problem.*

*Each time the survey was completed and the results shared with the executive, two things occurred. The executive leading the process would go through the anonymous comments and guess who might have written some of the more negative ones. Rather than consider the comment and what might be done at a leadership level to make improvements, the comment was attributed to some employee who was forevermore deemed a negative employee. Coincidentally, some of these employees didn't last long in the organization. I observed this firsthand and wondered why negative comments were so quickly dismissed as coming from a negative source, but there was no reflection on what the comment might mean or how to make improvements in that particular area.*

*The second thing that occurred was the executive would find the team with the lowest engagement score and try to determine what was wrong with them. Some were sent to team workshops. In many cases, the manager was brought into the executive's office to discuss what was wrong with their team. I know this because one year, I was the one brought into that office. At the time, I was managing the most effective communications team I had ever had the pleasure of working with. We were a small group and we all got along really well, despite the fact that we were very different. We had very open and honest communication. We were productive and even took on many tasks that were outside our area of responsibility. The challenges we faced weren't within the team but rather a result of not being brought in on things in a timely manner in order to effectively do our jobs.*

*For example, in a meeting of senior leaders that I had managed to invite myself to, one of the executives talked about a big announcement that was to be shared with her division that day. I was taken by surprise. As the person in charge of employee communication, I had no idea this announcement was being made. I felt blindsided and frustrated when a senior manager looked over to me to ask if perhaps this was something that needed to be shared with the whole company. I wasn't prepared to answer and was left looking like an idiot, one who had to beg to be at the table and then was unable to demonstrate why she deserved to be there. This happened regularly and contributed to the frustration of the communications department, which was reflected in our employee survey results.*

*It didn't occur to this executive that perhaps it wasn't the team that had the problem, but rather their senior leadership. I observed firsthand some of the other teams that landed at the bottom of the survey (relative to other teams, when, in fact, the results were still very positive) throughout the years. What I noticed was good communication, collaboration and overall good morale. They treated each other with respect and were very effective at getting their work done. On the other hand, they felt frustrated with senior leadership who created roadblocks to their ability to do their jobs effectively.*

*Over time, as the executive continued this practice, the employees learned how to respond to the survey to avoid being penalized for telling the truth. Because employees didn't think they were being heard and wanted to avoid being labelled or forced to participate in workshops to improve a team they already felt was highly functional, they began to practice what I've heard called 'five to stay alive.' On a Likert scale of one to five where five represents the most positive scenario or response, employees would answer five. Not everyone did this, but seasoned employees and teams who had been the object of the culture witch hunt, learned how to stay out of trouble.*

*The result was a huge blind spot for executives. While the results of the culture survey were impressive, the actual lived experience of the employees wasn't aligned to the results. Even worse was that the culture that was created was one of fear and mistrust.*

*The executive team had the best intentions. They truly wanted a constructive corporate culture where employees would thrive. They went to great lengths to achieve this. They cared deeply about the people who worked for them. Yet, even with the best intentions, without self-awareness and the willingness to look in the mirror to determine what could be done better, they never really achieved the ideal culture they were working towards.*

## CONTRIBUTING TO CULTURE

If you want to create a particular culture within your team or organization, there are a number of areas you will need to focus on.

### Policies and processes

Consider whether or not the things you do and the way you do them are in line with the culture you want to create. For example, a company states safety is their number one value. To say it isn't enough. This company also created and implemented policies, processes and procedures, such as regular meetings, checklists, training and reporting, that supported this culture of safety. Furthermore, employees were encouraged to bring up anything they felt could be done more safely. Safety was also audited annually and leaders were constantly reminding employees about safety.

## Desired behaviours and enforcing accountability

When you define the culture you want, you must also be clear about what that looks like on a day-to-day basis. Your company may want a culture of respect. Respect is a broad term and shows up in different ways. For example, if you respect other people's time, you won't be late for meetings. When you're specific about the desired and acceptable behaviours, you make it clear to employees how they should behave. When they behave the way you expect them to, you begin to create the culture you desire.

In the same vein, it helps to be clear about what is not acceptable behaviour. You can create expectations around what is acceptable and unacceptable behaviour, but it won't matter unless you hold people accountable. This is very important, because culture is not created through what you say but rather by what you do.

If people are not held accountable to behave in a way that contributes to a positive culture, the result will be a culture of whatever behaviours are accepted. When people are allowed to demonstrate disrespectful behaviour without consequence, the culture becomes one of disrespect. A company can say they want a culture of transparency. However, if people in the company withhold information, that culture will never come to fruition. There must be congruency between what leaders in the company say and what they do.

## KERI'S EXPERIENCE

*I once worked in an organization where senior leadership said they had a fair culture where everyone had the same opportunities. However, on several occasions, they appointed people into positions rather than going through a fair recruitment process.*

*An external consultant was offered a newly created senior management position without any kind of competition. My manager at the time was looking for an opportunity to grow with the company but because it was a relatively small organization, opportunities were few and far between. I would guess she wasn't the only person waiting for an opportunity for advancement. In her case, she got tired of waiting and left for another organization. Whether or not the person who was hired was the best for the job is irrelevant. The message that was sent to employees was the opposite of what the leaders said about fairness.*

*There were also 'favourites'—employees who were given opportunities others weren't. Again, a senior management position was created and handed to an individual, rather than having a fair process where anyone interested had the opportunity to apply for the new position. This was obvious to the other employees, who did not see the culture as fair but rather as one of favouritism. The result was mistrust in leadership. Another unintended consequence was that other employees doubted the new leader's capabilities because she was handed the position as opposed to winning it over others.*

*While the issue of the unfair process of promotion and hiring came up in employee survey comments, the practice continued to occur and some senior managers even tried to justify it.*

If what leaders say is not congruent with the behaviours they demonstrate, employees will mistrust what is said. When there is no trust in leadership, there can never be a constructive culture where employees are fully engaged.

## Corporate rhetoric

Without aligned behaviours, words mean nothing. However, it is still important for an organization to set cultural expectations and tell people what is expected of them. This can be done a number of ways. The mission, vision and values set the tone for the organization. If they are done well, they provide clarity to employees about what they must do and how. Any kind of employee communication can reinforce the desired culture and the acceptable behaviours that contribute to this, such as content on the intranet, signage on the walls throughout the building, or content in CEO presentations.

Leaders in the organization must also contribute to sharing these expectations through conversations with employees and play a significant role in communicating with employees. Employees put more trust in what their bosses tell them as opposed to what might come through corporate communications. That means, as a leader, you have a responsibility to take those corporate messages, share them with your team and help them to figure out what that information means for them and their jobs within the organization.

## The stories that are told

One of the ways to share these expectations is through the stories shared within the organization. Consider this from an anthropological perspective. Storytelling is used in many societies to pass on values and traditions and contribute to culture. Positive behaviours should be recognized and celebrated through stories. This reinforces those behaviours and encourages others to behave in a similar manner.

An absence of communication also contributes to culture. What is shared and what is kept secret contributes to culture. Stories will be shared regardless of a company's willing participation in cultivating them. 'Water-cooler talk' or gossip among employees will take place where there are gaps of information. That's why leaders can contribute to a positive culture when they fill those gaps with the real story.

Consider how you publicly recognize those who demonstrate the desired behaviours of collaboration. You need to recognize the people and teams who work collaboratively. Conversely, you should not publicly recognize those who do not work well with others, even though they may excel in other areas, such as remarkable sales numbers. The behaviours and stories that are celebrated and shared within the company are what people will aspire to.

## Social responsibility

Social responsibility includes the investments an organization makes in the community in which employees live and work. However, it also includes a number of other things, such as how employees are treated and compensated, how you address environmental and economic sustainability, how ethically a company operates, how shareholders are treated and compensated, and how suppliers are selected and managed. Just as within an organization, the behaviours demonstrated with all other stakeholders contributes to corporate culture. Behaviours, more than words, contribute to corporate culture, whether through interactions with employees or any other stakeholders.

## Leader behaviours

An organization can have all the above contributors to corporate culture in place, but if leaders do not demonstrate the desired or acceptable behaviours, the desired culture will never exist. Leader behaviours are the most integral piece of corporate culture. What leaders say must unequivocally align with what they do. Employees are watching.

## KERI'S EXPERIENCE

*I worked with an organization that promoted work-life balance. They offered a number of attractive perks to support employees in this way. They provided a generous number of personal days and benefits for employee wellness. They had a policy in place for employees to work compressed work weeks, an option where employees could put in longer days to earn a day off every so often. As a mother, this was incredibly helpful for me. While I have a great husband who is very helpful, his job doesn't offer a lot of flexibility and I still carry the majority of the responsibilities when it comes to our children. An extra day off every so often gave me some time to run errands, take the kids to appointments, and sometimes, just have some time alone for myself.*

*I was effective in my role and very efficient with my time, putting in extra hours when it was necessary to make sure deadlines were met. I found it easy to achieve my business results while also working a compressed work week. I wasn't taking more time off work; I just compressed my time into fewer days.*

*When I had the opportunity to step into a senior leadership role, my new boss suggested I give up the compressed work schedule. Apparently, my physical absence from the office one day a month might look bad for someone who was a senior leader. As a leader I was to support others to take advantage of work-life balance policies, but I wasn't supposed to do so myself.*

*The message was that work-life balance is important for employees BUT if you want to get ahead in the company, you will need to sacrifice this work-life balance.*

*In the end, we agreed I could continue my compressed schedule and we would reassess after a couple of months. When I was able to demonstrate my continued effectiveness without consequence, I was allowed to continue with the compressed schedule. I met deadlines and made time for my employees. I was also able to demonstrate to employees that balance was important and could be achieved even at a senior leadership level.*

The behaviours of the leaders trump all the other strategies and tactics a company may put in place to create a positive corporate culture. If the leaders can't or won't walk the talk, no one else will.

To achieve a constructive culture, and therefore increased productivity and profitability, leaders must create a safe place where employees can thrive. The best leaders are the best because they care about the success of the people on their team.

People need to feel like they belong. They also need to feel safe; not just physically safe, but psychologically safe. When people feel psychologically safe, they trust there will be no negative repercussions for voicing their ideas, questions, concerns, or mistakes. In 2015, Google released the results of a two-year study of its teams. What they found was that psychological safety was the single most important factor impacting performance. Individuals on teams with higher psychological safety were more engaged. That engagement, in turn, leads to better performance.

As a leader, this is where your behaviours and relationships make a difference. Consider how you are meeting the needs of your employees.

- Have you built trusting relationships with your team?
- Is your communication with your employees two-way?
- Is there mutual respect?
- How do you contribute to their feelings of belonging?
- How often do you connect with individual employees?
- Do you create formal and informal ways to connect with your employees?
- Are you congruent in what you say and what you do?

People need to know they matter, that what they have to say is important, and the work they do is valued. They need to be assured of this recurrently. You can achieve this by regularly recognizing employees for their efforts in big and small ways. You can give them autonomy in how they carry out their work and empower them to make decisions.

Furthermore, when people find meaning and purpose in their work, when they're able to learn and grow, they are more likely to work to their potential. Leaders can nurture this by frequently communicating the mission or purpose of the organization and how an employee's work fits in. Offer employees formal and informal opportunities to learn and grow. Some people think they need to give an employee a promotion to make them happy, but the truth is, they could be just as happy if they had the opportunity to work on a special project or if they were invited to contribute in a meeting they wouldn't normally be invited to. Offer your employees honest feedback with the intent of helping them become better. Help your employees become comfortable with the unknown because they know you have their best interests at heart.

Culture is complicated and it takes a significant amount of work to create a constructive culture where employees are engaged and thriving. However, it is possible to create the desired culture and the results will be higher productivity and profitability.

## ■ REFLECTION QUESTIONS ■

1.  How would I describe the culture within my team? My organization? (Be honest with yourself. You don't have to share this with anyone else.)

2.  Does the actual culture align with corporate rhetoric? For example, does what the leaders in the organization say align with their actions?

3.  What behaviours do I demonstrate that contribute to a positive culture?

4.  What behaviours do I demonstrate that may have a negative impact on culture?

5.  Does what I do on a regular basis align with what I expect from my employees? If not, what will I do about it?

6.  How do I create psychological safety in my team?

7.  Do I, as a leader, have meaning or purpose in my work? Am I learning and growing? And if not, what do I need so I can be the best leader for my team?

## Importance of a Mentor

"Getting the most out of life isn't about how much you keep for yourself, but how much you pour into others."

David Stoddard, author of *The Heart of Mentoring: Ten Proven Principles for Developing People to Their Fullest Potential*

### WHO DESERVES A MENTOR?

No one *needs* a mentor, but everyone deserves one. If you do not have a mentor today, search one out and start the process. Having a mentor is one of the most valuable and rewarding experiences you will do for your leadership and personal development.

### DOUG'S EXPERIENCE

*I look at where I am in my career as a leader and I see the influence of the numerous mentors I have had throughout my life. I am fortunate to have been touched by many willing to offer me advice, guidance, and, most importantly, an example of leadership.*

## FORMAL OR AD HOC

Many choose to have a formal relationship with a mentor where they meet regularly and have structured interactions. Often the week or month between sessions is debriefed, goals are set, tasks are identified, and progress is measured. This fits many mentor's needs, as they are often busy with time a premium. Formal relationships provide dedicated time, often with measurable goals and activities, to be carried out between sessions.

Less formal relationships are also extremely valuable, and some prefer those to structured sessions. They can take the form of engagement when you are about to encounter a meeting, decision, or major project, or are focusing on a specific issue. They can be an unstructured check-in with no agenda, or a customized process that fits your style and that of your mentor. In the end, it is important to choose a structure that works for you and your mentor.

## CHOOSING A MENTOR

It is important not to fall into the trap of choosing someone just like you. Choosing a mentor is an opportunity to learn from those who are experienced or have mastered skills outside of your area of expertise or comfort level. This is an opportunity to broaden your horizons and draw on those who have been involved in areas you may not have had the opportunity to be exposed to. Look for those who have a noticeable approach or skill set different from yours. In addition, look for someone who has influence with others, those that have clearly developed interpersonal skills that have helped them to become successful. Your mentor should have experience and interest in developing others and be willing to provide honest and helpful feedback and, above all, is a terrific listener.

Finding a mentor is often much easier than you may expect. There are many terrific leaders out there who are extremely willing to share their skills, knowledge, and experience—they are simply waiting to be asked.

## DON'T EXPECT ONE MENTOR TO BE YOUR EVERYTHING

Everyone has an area or areas they are extremely competent in, but it will be difficult to find a mentor that can support you in all areas. You may find it valuable to find multiple mentors who have unique and different skill sets. You may recognize you need mentorship with specific human-resource or labour relations issues, or political acuity, building a team, dealing with conflict, or a number of other areas you require support or would like to develop.

Be aware that some mentors will contradict each other. This is normal, providing you with a balanced experience. When you have alternating perspectives from your mentors, you will need to make a choice. At the end of the day, 'go with the gut' as to which mentor is providing the best advice for that particular issue you are dealing with.

## DON'T FORGET TO KEEP THE CORE YOU

Remember that it is your skills and actions that have brought you to this level of success in your career. Be careful not to carve off the elements of your work and leadership style that has carried you this far. Use the feedback and experience of the mentor to complement your core strengths and challenge yourself to look at areas that can use tweaks, refinements, or adjustments, but don't tear down your framework.

## CUTTING THE TIES

If the mentor relationship is not working for you and you have given the relationship a fair opportunity, then thank them and move on. Your time is valuable as is the time of your mentor, so do not waste their time or yours. Ensure the reason for moving on is not that you simply are uncomfortable with being challenged. If the mentor is not challenging you from time to time, then they likely are not getting the full potential from you.

## STAY ENGAGED AND CONNECTED

You will find many of your mentors will become lifelong connections. They will be extremely interested in you and how your leadership style develops, even taking pride in seeing and hearing about your successes and accomplishments. Don't forget to share your experiences that have been shaped by their mentoring.

## DOUG'S EXPERIENCE

*I never formalized my mentoring relationship with those that shaped my career and 'mentored' me, but I have grown so much from those around me. My mentors have been subordinates, peers, supervisors, and others that I respect. My mentors have been diverse in their backgrounds, experiences, and roles. I have learned from these great leaders by watching, listening and engaging with them on a variety of topics.*

*In one case, a very senior leader made a critical error in the message that was delivered to staff. It was clearly portrayed in a manner that led people to believe A when it was actually B. Although not immediately, that person recognized the impact of this message, and took ownership and clarified the message to all staff. She owned it, she was vulnerable and they fixed it. I have never forgotten that situation and have tried to model my behaviour after that example.*

*Another mentor of mine stood out as he always focused on the people. He was a hard driver, results focused, very professional and highly demanding, but always prioritized the team. In one case, a young employee was caring for his dying spouse. My mentor recognized that the employee had used up all his paid leave and was struggling with deciding if he needed to take a leave without pay. The mentor immediately provided calm to that person and ensured they had all the flexibility they needed to carry out their primary task of caring for a loved one. That is a gift the employee will never forget and will always be grateful for. I have tried to model my behaviour as a leader in the same way, always focusing on the people first.*

*Yet another mentor ensured those who showed promise and were deserving by their performance and attitude were given additional opportunity to grow and challenge themselves beyond what was readily available. I was the beneficiary of that support but also watched that mentor support so many others throughout their careers.*

*The point here is that I have learned so much from mentors that I will never be able to repay. As indicated, much of what I have learned from mentors was simply from my watching them as they modelled behaviour. (Thank you, Len, Bill, Martin, Bob, Jim, Dave, Murray and Lori. I appreciate your time and mentorship.)*

## HOW TO GET THE MOST OUT OF MENTORING

Use the opportunity of mentorship to its fullest to try new things, to stretch yourself, and to seek as much feedback and observations of others as you can. Invest in this as you would with any other opportunity. Listen with an open mind, ask many questions, and put aside your ego as you search for what you can learn from the experience of your mentor. This can truly be one of the most rewarding pieces of your development that you will partake in.

## RETURN THE GIFT

It is important to your staff and organization—and actually your responsibility as a leader—to give back. Take the time to let others know you are willing to provide mentorship. Reach out to friends and colleagues or during interactions in courses or seminars. Many mentors wait to be asked. Don't wait, reach out, be proactive, and seek out someone to mentor. It may be one of the most rewarding services you provide in your career.

## ■ REFLECTION QUESTIONS ■

1. Who was the best mentor I have had and why? How were they unique or special as a mentor?

2. What would I like to learn from a mentor?

3. If I have not reached out for mentorship, what is holding me back?

4. What are my expectations of a mentor? What do I want to learn from the relationship?

5. How will I ensure I get the most out of a mentorship relationship?

6. What do I think a mentor expects from me?

# MIND THE GAP

# The Value of Coaching

> **"A coach is someone who tells you what you don't want to hear, who has you see what you don't want to see, so you can be who you have always known you could be."**
>
> *Tom Landry, Football coach*

An effective leader is always learning. This is absolutely necessary because the world is always changing. Your industry is evolving, tools you use to do your job and deliver your products and services are changing, and the people who work for you are changing. If you are not growing and learning as a leader, you will quickly become ineffective, or worse,—irrelevant.

## KERI'S EXPERIENCE

*Several years ago, I started working for a new boss. My role hadn't changed but the structure of the company did. At the time, I was reporting directly to an executive vice president, which made my job easier. Often Corporate Communications is brought in after decisions are made, which means the work we do to disseminate information is very tactical rather than strategic. Having direct access and reporting to the executive allowed me to be in the loop early and therefore more strategic.*

*When the structure changed, an Associate VP was added between me and the executive I had been reporting to. We had a very difficult start to our relationship. I'll take half the blame because I was not happy to have this additional layer inserted above me. However, this new AVP, who had been in management for decades, also contributed to our rocky relationship. For the first six months, we met only casually on a few occasions. We had no formal meetings. I received little direction or information from him, never mind any vision or inspiration.*

*I grew more and more frustrated until one day the frustration burst out of me in an embarrassing display of tears during a meeting with my peers, the AVPs in our division, and the Executive VP. It was not my finest moment. Afterwards my boss and I had a very long heart to heart. He admitted he had failed me as a leader. He also told me he had previous employees who told him he was the best boss they'd ever had. For me, he had been one of the worst.*

In this example, the AVP stopped growing and learning as a leader. He assumed that because he was once a great boss, he would always be a great boss. There are many ways leaders can continue to grow. One of those ways is by using an executive coach.

## WHAT IS EXECUTIVE COACHING?

An executive coach is trained to work with individuals (or teams) to unlock their potential. Through conversations and questions, a coach helps individuals to clarify goals and work toward their objectives. Coaches provide a confidential and safe space for leaders to reflect and increase their self-awareness.

## WHAT COACHING IS NOT

There are other relationships that, at first glance, may seem like coaching but are not. Each of these are effective for different reasons, but it's important to make the distinction between coaching and counselling, mentoring or consulting.

Counselling is focused on understanding and resolving the past to support individuals to be well in the present. Counsellors deal with issues, such as trauma, abuse, addictions and bad relationships that may cause dysfunction or mental illness. They provide tools and support to help people move from dysfunctional to functional.

Coaches, on the other hand, do not work to resolve dysfunction but rather to enhance an individual's ability to achieve their potential. Their work is future focused.

Mentoring is another relationship similar to coaching and is also very valuable in leadership development. A mentor is generally someone with plenty of knowledge and experience who is willing to share what they know. You can learn from their successes as well as their mistakes and forge your own path. While coaches may have similar experience and knowledge, which they may sometimes share in coaching conversations, they partner with you to support you to find your own way to address challenges and achieve your goals.

Finally, consulting can seem similar to coaching. Consultants are typically hired to fill a skill or resource gap. Leaders rely on consultants for their expertise and advice. In a coaching relationship, the expertise comes from you and the process comes from the coach.

## WHY WOULD YOU WANT TO USE A COACH?

Like many leaders, you're probably very busy. There are demands on your time and attention and results you're expected to achieve, not to mention a personal life and your own wellness. It's easy to go about each day ticking off boxes on your endless to do list. But how often do you actually take the time to think about all those boxes? Are they the right boxes in the right order? Coaching is an opportunity for reflection and focus. It can help you take a step back and analyze your challenges and opportunities and discover the best way to address or seize them. It can help you increase your productivity and become more effective.

It can be lonely at the top. There are few people you can confide in or bounce ideas off. The higher you are within the organizational structure, the less likely it is you'll get honest feedback from those who report to you. No one wants to tell the boss they're doing a bad job. A coach can facilitate 360° feedback where your employees and colleagues provide anonymous feedback to your coach who identifies themes and shares the feedback with you. They'll also work with you to make changes and grow based on what you've heard.

## KERI'S EXPERIENCE

*When I first started managing a team, I demonstrated some pretty good leadership (if I do say so myself). My team seemed happy and productive. At the time I was entering into the Master of Arts in Leadership program at Royal Roads University and I was required to go through an exercise where I gathered feedback from three of my colleagues. From that feedback, a common theme emerged. To grow my leadership ability, I needed to empower others to take on leadership roles. When I reflected on the feedback, I realized that, while I might have been doing a good job of leading a team, there was an opportunity for me to become a better leader. I was then able to identify opportunities to empower the employees on my team to demonstrate their leadership, which made them even more effective and engaged.*

People are creatures of habit. Our brains are designed that way. Change is hard. Coaches can help by offering a safe place for reflection. Through conversations, coaches can help you reveal your blind spots. Everyone has them. Once you accept that as fact, you'll be willing to address them.

## WHAT TO LOOK FOR IN A COACH?

Like any profession, there are good and not so good coaches. When you invest time and resources into a coaching relationship, you want to make sure you're getting value. Here are some things to look for.

Training: coach training has come a long way and there are programs offered by reputable universities. There are also many other programs that are excellent but not run by an educational institution. One way to ensure the training is legitimate is to see if it is recognized by a professional association such as the International Coaching Federation (ICF).

Certification: these professional associations also offer certification to coaches, which might include a training requirement, specified hours of coaching experience, exams or other requirements for a coach to become certified. While not being certified doesn't necessarily mean someone isn't a good coach, certification provides some assurance that a coach has met certain standards.

Authenticity and honesty: If you're going to make an investment in coaching, you probably don't want someone wasting your time beating around the bush. Difficult feedback is not easy to deliver (or receive) but it's important for your personal growth. To get the most out of your investment, find a coach who will be straight with you.

Trust and connection: To get the most out of coaching, you have to allow yourself to be vulnerable so it's important you find a coach who understands you and you feel you can trust. Take time to find the right coach. Most coaches will provide a free introductory meeting. During this time, you will get to know each other. Ask the potential coach about her coaching style and experience. Then trust your gut. If you don't feel comfortable with this person, move on.

## COACHING WORKS

You'd expect this book, written by coaches, to plug coaching. Coaching is a great tool for leadership development, but you don't have to take our word for it. While research about the positive impact of coaching isn't as abundant as other areas, the research that does exist is positive. Here are some examples:

- International Coach Federation (ICF) presented research indicating coaching tends to generate an ROI of between $4 and $8 for every dollar invested. (Grenier, 2018)
- Coaching assisted in the development of three main competencies: leadership behavior (82%), building teams (41%), and developing staff. (36%) (Parker-Wilkins, 2006)
- 55% of the participants increased leadership effectiveness as rated by others. 52% increased as rated by self. (Thach, 2002)
- 98% percent of coaching clients said, "My coach helped me identify specific behaviors that would help me achieve my goals." (Center for Creative Leadership study, 2016)
- 66% percent of people who received effective coaching reported a positive impact on their performance and job satisfaction. (BlessingWhite Consulting, 2015)
- 88% of managers said coaching helped them achieve their goals. (BlessingWhite Consulting, 2015)

## ▨ REFLECTION QUESTIONS ▨

Working with a coach is most effective when you're committed to making a change for yourself.

1. How could I benefit from working with a coach?

2. What goals do I have that I could use some support to achieve?

3. If I received feedback from my colleagues and employees, how might I become a better leader?

4. What leadership skills would I like to enhance with the help of a coach?

# Continuous Growth

**"We must never be too busy to take
time to sharpen the saw."**

*Stephen Covey*

As a leader, it is vital that you continue to evolve and grow. It is critical that you place yourself in areas where you are challenged and required to think and open your mind. Many leaders, who were once capable, contributing key players, became stagnant and out of touch because they failed to "sharpen their saw" throughout their career. They relied on their experience alone and were left behind in an environment that was continuously changing. To be successful and relevant they needed to ensure they were continuously growing— at the very least—keeping current with their knowledge, skill and abilities. The world is continuously changing with new science, technology, knowledge, theories and social expectations that require workplaces to continually evolve. If leaders don't evolve as well, they quickly become ineffective and irrelevant. New situations and circumstances arrive daily. The COVID 19 pandemic, for example, was a situation leaders never had to address before. Only leaders who were able to grow and adapt in the situation could continue to be effective.

## DOUG'S EXPERIENCE

*I have been fortunate throughout my career to develop, grow and maintain my positive enthusiasm because I was exposed to a number of different sections and positions within my organization. Many people are successful at ensuring continuous growth within the same role or position, but I needed to shift roles or 'space' to do this.*

Some believe continuous growth has to be in the form of formal courses or education, but some of the best examples of personal growth occur when team members expose themselves to experiences that ensure they stay current and viable for the team they are part of. An example of this is capturing opportunities to collaborate and brainstorm ideas, which is a great way to learn and to grow from others. The phrase, "you don't know what you don't know" demonstrates why collaboration and brainstorming with others can stretch our professional growth.

There are many areas of opportunity for growth in one's career and life in general. Never stop looking for something that interests you, scares you, or you know you need to work on.

## DOUG'S EXPERIENCE

*One example of my growth began early in my career when I became part of the hiring process, including interview panels. I decided this was an area that both interested me and would benefit me in my career. I jumped at every opportunity to be part of a panel. Although this endeavor took me away from my base work extensively, my manager saw the big picture in my development and the benefit to the organization and supported me in this growth.*

*I saw this as an opportunity to choose future leaders and shape my organization. I soon realized being part of the selection panels was also a massive opportunity for my own growth. I was able to witness some of the best candidate interviews and, quite frankly, those that could use some work. I learned from all of them. It was my opportunity to see those that 'rocked' the interview, and those that perhaps had the skills, but did not properly display them to the panel in a confident manner. I did my own research on new and innovative assessment tools, I looked back at previous interviews to see what worked and what could be built upon. I volunteered for interview panels with other organizations to learn from how they conducted their interviews. I ensured that our interviews were conducted in the manner that our HR department required them to be, and when their process did not make sense, I was a vehicle for change and advancement of what was industry standard and best practices for interviews.*

As an aspiring leader, take the opportunity for temporary assignments, for coaching and mentoring opportunities, and for job shadowing. And as an experienced leader, make sure to provide these opportunities to others. Far too often supervisors have their peers act in their positions when they are away, rather than providing the opportunity to others who are aspiring to that role.

Your growth may be achieved by following inspirational leaders or experts in a particular field. You may find your inspiration from LinkedIn articles, or twitter posts, or podcasts. Quite frankly it does not matter where you find your inspiration as long as you find it.

As a leader, funding and supporting staff development is one of the greatest investments you will ever make. If you are a decision maker in your organization, dedicate time, effort and resources to training that can provide meaningful, credible and applicable development to your teams.

Many organizations have extensive formal education programs or provide financial support for post secondary education. For example, the BC Public Service is a leader in encouraging staff growth by providing financial support for a number of post-secondary programs. Those programs have the ability to benefit the BC Public Service by growing their employees. The growth for the employees is beyond the formal learning, it is also about the exposure to others. Those contacts and that shared learning are invaluable to the employee's personal growth.

## ■ REFLECTION QUESTIONS ■

1. What does continuous growth mean to me?

2. Why is it important for me to continue to grow as a leader?

3. What has been the most meaningful example of growth I have seen in my leadership development?

4. What areas of growth am I excited about embarking on?

5. What is holding me back?

# MIND THE GAP

# ■ Conclusion ■

Leadership is all about people—how to motivate and inspire them to achieve the results your organization is looking for. People are complicated. They're emotional and sometimes unpredictable. All people want to be seen, heard and understood. They also want to feel like they're making a contribution and are valued for the work they do. Whatever role you had before you were promoted to supervisor likely did not prepare you for all the challenges that come with leadership.

Supervisors need to be aware of the gap between being an employee and being a supervisor. They must work to develop the new skills they need to be a successful leader. Many new leaders struggle or even fail because they are not equipped with the skills required to lead people. Many organizations will promote people into leadership positions without any kind of training to prepare them for this very different role. This leaves new leaders on their own. Sometimes these new leaders will continue to focus on what they've been good at and continue to be that subject matter expert rather than focusing on leadership.

Leadership is as much about you as it is about the people who are following you. It's about knowing who you are, your strengths and weaknesses and what is most important to you. In order to take care of others, you must first take care of yourself. Finally, you must have the courage to look at yourself to understand the impact you have on others.

Leadership requires constant and continuous learning. The people you lead are changing. Different generations have diverse needs and expectations of their jobs and their leaders. People from different walks of life or cultures will have various perspectives or face unique challenges. The environment in which you lead is continuously evolving. Technology constantly changes, new regulations are being enforced, and things like a pandemic can impact the way you do business. If you do not look at leadership as a journey, where constant learning is required, you will soon become ineffective and irrelevant.

As you continue your leadership journey, here is one more opportunity for reflection.

- What new things did I learn while reading this book?
- What leadership ideas or strategies did I already know but was reminded of their importance to my leadership?
- What new ideas will I implement in my leadership?
- Where are my opportunities to grow as a leader?
- What can I do to grow in these areas?
- What have I learned about myself as I read through this book?

Maya Angelou, poet, once said, "People will forget the things you do, and people will forget the things you say. But people will never forget how you made them feel." She wasn't the first to say something along these lines. Similar quotes have been attributed to others. This speaks to the relevancy of the idea. So, as a last reflection, consider this:

*As a leader, consider,*
*how do I want to make people feel?*

# ◼ Appendix A ◼

# Communications Strategy Template (from Chapter 10)

**Background** - What is the context within which you are communicating? What has happened? Why do you need to communicate?

**Considerations** - Are there any circumstances that should be considered? Are there any sensitivities around what is to be communicated?

**Communication Objectives** - What do you want your audience to feel, think or do?

**Target Audiences** - Who are your primary and secondary audiences? Are you addressing internal and external audiences? What are their information needs?

**Key Messages** - Develop key messages for each target audience you want to communicate to. Keep in mind what you want them to feel, think or do.

Communication Tactics - How will you share your message? Whether you're communicating once or several times over months, consider how you will share your message. Some tactics are included below.

## INTERNAL COMMUNICATIONS

- Face-to-face meeting
- Email
- Intranet
- Events
- Conference calls
- Webinars

# EXTERNAL COMMUNICATIONS

## Online

- Email
- Website(s)
- Social Media
- Multimedia: such as Screensavers, wallpaper, or online games
- E-newsletter

## Media

- Media release
- Radio, television, print
- Editorial
- Letter to the editor
- Features

## Advertising

- Print
- Direct mail
- Billboards
- Radio
- Television

## Print

- Brochures
- Posters
- Leaflets
- Reports

## Public Relations

- Event/Stunt
- Endorsements
- Conferences

Timelines and Responsibility - When will each tactic be delivered? Who will prepare (write and design) the content? Who will deliver the content (e.g., the CEO will speak at an in-person meeting)?

Budget - How much money is available for preparation and delivery of communication tactics? Your budget will determine whether some tactics can be delivered.

Evaluating success - How will you know if your communication has been effective? What performance indicators and evaluating measures will you use? These could be quantitative (e.g., sales increased by 5%, 57 people attended the event) or qualitative (there was good engagement during employee meetings). It's important to assess your strategy throughout so changes can be made if necessary.

- Have you achieved your objectives (e.g., create awareness, change behaviour)?
- Did your audience do what had to be done?
- Did you use the right tools?
- Did you come in on budget?

# ◼ References ◼

## CHAPTER 1

Maxwell, John. (2021/August 7th). Are you really leading, or are you just taking a walk? *John C. Maxwell Blog.* https://www.johnmaxwell.com/blog/are-you-really-leading-or-are-you-just-taking-a-walk/

Kotter, John. (2013/January 9). Management Is (Still) Not Leadership. *Harvard Business Review.* https://hbr.org/2013/01/management-is-still-not-leadership

Covey, Stephen R. (2004). *The 7 Habits of Highly Effective People: Powerful Lessons in Personal Change.* New York, NY: The Free Press.

Bobinski, Dan. (2014/February 16). The Difference Between Management and Leadership. *Management Issues - at the heart of changing workplace.* https://www.management-issues.com/opinion/1125/the-difference-between-management-leadership

## CHAPTER 3

Harvard Business School. (2012, May 24). *Sheryl Sandberg Addresses the Class of 2012* [Video]. YouTube. https://www.youtube.com/watch?v=2Db0_RafutM&feature=youtu.be

## CHAPTER 4

Sandberg, S., & Scovell, N. (2019). *Lean in: Women, Work, and the Will to Lead,* New York: Alfred A. Knopf (Random House)

## CHAPTER 5

Chamine, Shirzad. (2016). *Positive Intelligence: Why Only 20% of Teams and Individuals Achieve Their True Potential.* Austin TX: Greenleaf Book Group Press.

Freedman, J. (2021, June 3). *5 Questions to Develop Your Empathy/ Increase Empathy for Success* [Video]. YouTube. https://www.youtube. com/watch?v=X8CJUvwq8Og

Institute for Health Human Potential. *Executive Summary: The Business Case for Emotional Intelligence.* https://www.ihhp.com/ wp-content/uploads/WHITE-PAPER-ROI-for-Emotional-Intelligence.pdf

Freedom, J. (2002). *Emotional What? Definitions and History of EQ".* *Six Seconds' EQ TODAY* magazine. https://prodimages.6seconds. org/pdf/Emotional_WHAT.pdf

## CHAPTER 6

Baum, D., & Scullard, M. (2021). *Everything Disc Solutions.* Wiley. https://www.everythingdisc.com/.

Bradberry, T., & Greaves, J. (2009). *Emotional Intelligence 2.0.* TalentSmart.

Daniel Goleman (1995) cited in: John O. Dozier (2010) *The Weeping, the Window, the Way,* Tate Publishing, p. 130.

Goldsmith, M. (2007, January 22). Feed forward. https:// marshallgoldsmith.com/articles/1438/.

Myers, I. (1962). *The Myers Briggs type indicator: Manual.*

Riso, D. R. (1990). *Understanding the enneagram: The practical guide to personality types.* Boston: Houghton Mifflin.

Scudder, T. (2021, August 13). *SDI 2.0 methodology and meaning.* corestrengths.com. https://www.corestrengths.com/sdi-2-0-methodology-and-meaning

## CHAPTER 7

Chopra, Deepak M.D. (1994). *The Seven Spiritual Laws of Success.* Novato, California: Amber-Allen Publishing, New World Library.

## CHAPTER 8

Chamine, Shirzad. (2016). *Positive Intelligence: Why Only 20% of Teams and Individuals Achieve Their True Potential.* Austin TX: Greenleaf Book Group Press.

Topham, Gaynor. (2021). Don't Confuse Having a Life with a Career. *Sprout blog.* https://www.sproutnz.com/insights-blog/don-t-confuse-having-a-career-with-having-a-life/

## CHAPTER 9

Godin, Seth. (2014/February 23). The Most Important Question. *Seth Godin's Blog.* https://seths.blog/2014/02/the-most-important-question/

Covey, Stephen R. (2018). The Speed of Trust: The One Thing That Changes Everything. New York, NY: The Free Press.

## CHAPTER 11

Daskal, L. (2016, March 28). 100 answers to the question: *What is leadership? Inc.com.* https://www.inc.com/lolly-daskal/100-answers-to-the-question-what-is-leadership.html.

Tzu, L. (1996). *Tao Te Ching*

## CHAPTER 12

Ozick, C. (1983). *Art & ardor:* Essays. New York: Knopf.

## CHAPTER 14

Chodron, P. (2018). *The Places That Scare You: A Guide to Fearlessness in Difficult Times.* Boulder, Colorado: Shambhala.

## CHAPTER 15

Green, S. (2020, July 16). *Having tough conversations and making tough decisions.* https://shanegreen.com/having-tough-conversations-and-making-tough-decisions

## CHAPTER 16

Paul Foster, CEO The Business Therapist. *More than Engineering.* https://morethan-engineering.com/problem-employees

## CHAPTER 17

Khurana, Simran. (2021, September 8). *Quotes About Being Alone— but Not Lonely.* https://www.thoughtco.com/being-alone-is-not-necessarily-bad-2833074

## CHAPTER 18

Houston, E. (2020, December 28). *What is goal setting and how to do it well. PositivePsychology.com.* https://positivepsychology.com/goal-setting

Kassim, N. (2021, September 23). Steve Jobs's leadership style and what we can learn from it. *Idea Drop, Idea Management Software.* https://ideadrop.co/customer-success/steve-jobs-leadership-style-what-we-can-learn/#:~:text=%E2%80%9CIt%20doesn't%20make%20sense,tell%20us%20what%20to%20do.%E2%80%9D&text=Key%20takeaway%3A,in%20your%20company%20is%20important.&text=Jobs%20didn't%2C%20and%20that's,him%20such%20a%20roaring%20success

## CHAPTER 19

Covey, Stephen R. (2004). *The 7 Habits of Highly Effective People: Powerful Lessons in Personal Change.* New York, NY:The Free Press.

## CHAPTER 20

Bridges, W. (1991). *Managing transitions: Making the most of change.* Reading, Massachusetts: Addison-Wesley.

Hiatt, J. (2006). *ADKAR: A model for change in business, government, and our community.* Loveland, Colorado: Prosci Learning Center Publications.

Lewin, K. (1947) *Frontiers in Group Dynamics.* Human Relations, 1, 5-41. http://dx.doi.org/10.1177/001872674700100103

Prentice, A. E. (2013). *Leadership for the 21st century.* Santa Barbara: ABC-CLIO.

## CHAPTER 21

Ward, W. A. (1968). *Thoughts of a Christian optimist: The words of William Arthur Ward.* Anderson, S.C: Droke House; distributed by Grosset and Dunlap, New York.

University of London. *The story behind 'keep calm and carry on.'* University of London. https://london.ac.uk/about-us/history-university-london/story-behind-keep-calm-and-carry.

## CHAPTER 22

Schlitz, D. (1978). "The Gambler". {Recorded by K. Rogers] On the album, *The Gambler.* New York City, NY: United Artists.

## CHAPTER 23

Covey, Stephen. https://www.azquotes.com/quote/769672

## CHAPTER 24

Stoddard, David A. & Tamasy, Robert J. (2009). *The Heart of Mentoring: Ten Proven Principles for Developing People to Their Fullest Potential.* NavPress.

## CHAPTER 25

Deloitte Development LLC. (2012). *Core beliefs and culture Chairman's survey findings.* https://www2.deloitte.com/content/dam/Deloitte/global/Documents/About-Deloitte/gx-core-beliefs-and-culture.pdf

Gallup. (2021). *State of the Global Workplace 2021 Report*. Washington, D.C.

Gallup. (2017). *State of the Global Workplace 2017 Report*. Washington, D.C.

Kotter, J. P., and Heskett, J. L. (1992). *Corporate Culture and Performance*. New York: Free Press.

## CHAPTER 26

BlessingWhite Consulting, a Division of GP Strategies Corporation (2015). *Performance Management: Assess or Unleash*.

Duhigg, C. (2016, February 28). What Google Learned From Its Quest to Build the Perfect Team. *The New York Times Magazine,* page 20.

Grenier, N. (2018, August 29). Making the Business Case for Coaching. Association for Talent Development Article https://www.td.org/insights/making-the-business-case-for-executive-coaching.

Parker-Wilkins, Vernita. (2006). Business impact of executive coaching: Demonstrating monetary value. *Industrial and Commercial Training*, 38, 122-127.

Stawiski, S., Belzer, M. and Saas, R.G. (2016) Building the Case for Executive Coaching. *Center for Creative Leadership*

Thach, E. (2002). The Impact of Executive Coaching and 360 Feedback on Leadership Effectiveness. *Leadership & Organization Development Journal*, 23, 205–214.

## CHAPTER 27

Hill, J. (2018, July 28). Every great leader needs a coach. LinkedIn. https://www.linkedin.com/pulse/every-great-leader-needs-coach-dr-joseph-hill/?trk=related_artice_Every+Great+Leader+Needs+a+Coach_article-card_title.

Papatriantafillou, O. (2018, March 8). *Silent coaching*. LinkedIn. https://www.linkedin.com/pulse/silent-coaching-olga-papatriantafillou-m-a-/.

# Author Biographies

## DOUG FORSDICK

Doug is a dynamic leader who has built a career of continuous learning in the field of leadership. Doug is a public servant and operates Doug Forsdick Coaching and Consulting Services in Victoria, BC. As a Certified Executive Coach with ACC designation through the International Coaching Federation, Doug has coached many leaders at all levels from individuals preparing for their first job to Deputy Ministers.

Doug has over 35 years of leadership experience in his law enforcement career. As well, he has led numerous local, national and international boards and organizations. Doug believes in giving back to emerging leaders through mentorship, coaching and support.

Doug cares about those around him, holds himself and his team members to a high standard and always places a top priority on the sharing of knowledge and continuous learning.

Doug operates his coaching and consulting business in Victoria, British Columbia and lives with his wonderful girlfriend Anita on their rural property.

## What Doug's Clients and Employees Say About Him

*"Doug is a leader that cares about his people. He is someone that has always been respected by those around him. He has taught and mentored so many throughout his career. He is an asset to the public service."* - RK, Assistant Deputy Minister

*"Doug's coaching has been exactly what I needed to walk with me as I had several difficult decisions to make. He was there to challenge me, re-frame my situation and ultimately hold me capable of making decisions that I would not have had the confidence to make without his coaching. He has truly made a difference in my life."* - WT, Canadian Coast Guard

*"Doug is someone that truly understands leadership and accountability. He has a talent for always bringing out the best in those around him. He demands a great deal from his team but people want to work hard for Doug because he cares about people and he always looks after his team. I love that Doug always takes the time to share, teach and mentor those around him. Doug is an amazing leader that has shaped my career."* - BM, International Policing Expert

*"Doug is a compassionate and caring coach that truly helped me find the answers from within me. He has helped me to find my confidence again. The future is bright for me and I don't think I would have been able to get to this place without his help."* - DL, Big Brothers Big Sisters of Canada

# KERI SCHWEBIUS

Keri is an executive coach, speaker, leadership junkie and the founder and president of Ellevate Executive Coaching. Before becoming a Certified Executive Coach accredited with the International Coaching Federation (ICF), Keri completed two undergraduate degrees in French and Communications and spent more than 20 years in Public Relations helping executive teams communicate with stakeholders. During this time, she was a messenger and advisor for leaders. This led her to the field of leadership—as a leader herself, then empowering others to become leaders.

Keri's passion for leadership led her to complete a Masters of Arts in Leadership and a Graduate Certificate in Executive Coaching at Royal Roads University in Victoria, BC. She also holds accreditations in emotional intelligence, change management, communications and team building.

Today Keri helps leaders become more confident and effective resulting in increased personal performance, better employee engagement and effectiveness, and stronger business results.

Keri has a genuine desire to make a positive change in the world, working with individual and corporate clients, as the chair of the Saskatchewan chapter of Women in Leadership Foundation, and as the Chair of the Board of Directors of CityKidz Regina. Keri lives in Regina with her husband, Dean and three amazing Children.

Learn more at www.ellevatecoaching.com

## What Keri's clients say about her:

*"Keri has a passion for leadership and a commitment to making those around her better leaders. I have always admired her ability to connect with people, ask the right questions and to help people understand the opportunity to leverage their strengths and mitigate their weaknesses. She has certainly helped me become a better leader and I have witnessed her positive impact on organizations."* I.M., Chief People Officer

*"My work with Keri Schwebius has positively impacted my confidence and helped me build on my strengths and weaknesses. During our conversations, I work through the 'hairball' that is leadership to clearly identify root cause and defined actions I can take to hone my leadership skill. Since working with Keri, I have improved my own coaching skills which has empowered my team to improve their critical thinking and problem-solving skills. Keri has also improved my ability to manage stress and to focus on the things I can control and change. She has helped me assess situations and develop an approach to difficult conversations. Keri is someone you can confide in and learn from about yourself, your professional skills, your career ambitions, and your potential. She is genuine and real; someone I trust can help me continue to grow as a leader and a person."* J.C., Chief Strategy and Innovation Officer

*"Having Keri as my personal coach has given me great insight on how to become a better leader for my team. She has also given me tools to use in my new role and in my personal life. Keri is very pleasant to work with and I look forward to our meetings. Thank you, Keri for helping me along my journey."* L.H., Senior Administrative Assistant

# HEATHER THOMSON

Heather is an executive coach, positive intelligence coach, educational leader, and founder of Bold and Brave Coaching. She is the author of *"Lead By Design: A 30-Day Leadership Journey"* and a public speaker. Before becoming a Certified Executive Coach with her Associate Certified Coaching (ACC) designation from the International Coaching Federation and a Certified Positive Intelligence Coaching designation (CPQC), she worked in education for over 28 years and has held several leadership roles during that time. Currently she is working as a High School Administrator. She obtained a Masters in Educational Leadership and Administration and a Masters in Counselling Psychology. She also holds a Bachelor of Business Administration degree.

Heather is a wife, mother, educator, author, speaker and life and leadership coach. Her passion to support new and aspiring leaders has always guided her in her work with clients in order to help them become the leader that they strive to be. Her home is in Sherwood Park, Alberta with her husband, daughter, two dogs and their cat.

Heather is the chair of the Alberta chapter for Women In Leadership Foundation and a mentor for new and aspiring leaders in the Women In Leadership National Mentorship Program. She is also the chair for the Women In Leadership Elk Island Catholic Teachers.

To learn more visit Heather's website: www.boldandbravecoaching.com

## What clients say about Heather:

*"Heather has a wonderfully warm way of hearing who I am and supporting my journey towards work/life balance. As a busy mom of three with a demanding full-time career, life can be scattered and hectic; Heather has helped me find balance, calm, joy, and productivity. Her empowering approach brought me immediate benefits. She helped me tap into my strengths, set goals, and get things done."* L.M. - Assistant Principal, Alberta

*"The coaching sessions with Heather have provided me an opportunity to discuss my issues regarding my work expectations as a new leader to my organization. She also provided me with a greater sense of oversight and feedback regarding my leadership styles. I felt our sessions were always positive. Heather was a great coach and I truly appreciate her for her wisdom and strategic coaching techniques. I highly recommend Heather, to anyone needing clarity for career path direction. Spend time with Heather. Heather will listen and provide you great feedback. Feedback you can use to make yourself and those around you better at what you do."* G.K. Director, Government of British Columbia

*"My time with Heather can be described as transformational. I experienced breakthrough after breakthrough with her guidance. I grew both professionally and personally, and I'm so grateful for the time I was coached by Heather. Together, we created short-term goals to finish out the year, and also created long-term big picture goals for my future. After coaching with Heather, I can confidently say I know where I'm headed, and I couldn't be more excited for my future. Heather is warm and friendly, a great attentive listener, and a wonderful coach. She is able to really understand what is being said, and asks very intentional thought-provoking questions that lead to great moments of self discovery. If you want to experience powerful breakthroughs, Heather is the coach for you!"* J.F., Business Owner, Colorado

# ◼ Authors' Contact Information ◼

## DOUG FORSDICK

Doug.Forsdick@gmail.com

## KERI SCHWEBIUS

keri@ellevatecoaching.com
www.ellevatecoaching.com

## HEATHER THOMSON

boldandbravecoaching@gmail.com
www.boldandbravecoaching.com

Printed in Great Britain
by Amazon

79820054R00127